To Jackie,
Thank you for your
friendship!
Love Joyce

Finding the Pearls

Personal Stories & Reflections

Joyce Robitaille

To my husband, Roby
who has blessed me
with his never-ending support
and encouragement
and love as "big as the moon".

♥

Dwell, O Mind, Within Yourself

Dwell, O mind, within yourself;
Enter no other's home.
If you but seek there, you will find
All you are searching for.

God, the true Philosopher's Stone,
Who answers every prayer,
Lies hidden deep within your heart,
The richest gem of all.

How many pearls and precious stones
Are scattered all about
The outer court that lies before
The chamber of your heart!

A Song of Sri Ramakrishna

༄

Forward

My husband Roby, is fond of a poem called "The Dash" by Linda Ellis. On headstones we see two dates, the date of birth and the date of death with a dash between those years. When we remember a loved one who has passed, it isn't the day they were born or the day they died that is important. It is the time between those events that holds significance. To quote a verse from the poem:

> "For that dash represents all the time
> that they spent alive on earth.
> And now only those who loved them,
> know what that little line is worth."

What about our own "dash"? How are we living that time? Are we using that time in ways that serve ourselves and others in a positive way? Are we passionate about the things we do? Will those who know us remember the love we had for life and . . . for them? I don't know how much of my "dash" remains. But I hope to live it with enthusiasm and compassion. And that I am able to find the *many pearls and precious stones* that present themselves every day, even in the most mundane and sometimes most difficult circumstances

Joyce Robitaille

❧

Introduction

In my memoir, "Permission to Shine," I chronicled my life from my early adult years, through love, marriage and motherhood, through the illness and loss of my first husband, Lou, to the blessing of a second loving man in my life, Roby.

"Finding the Pearls" continues where the first one left off.   It sometimes reads like a story, but oftentimes it is more like a journal as I reflect on life as it happens.

ॐ

2012

"Some people want it to happen,
some wish it would happen,
others make it happen."

-Michael Jordan

If You Have a Burning Desire to Do Something. . . Do It!

There are two things I have always wanted to do. One was to write a novel. Problem was, every time I'd try to come up with a story line, it was my own. And for years, this is what prevented me from writing a story. I have no imagination, was always my excuse. But, I thought, what if I *write* my own story? Then maybe my mind will be clear and I can actually write that novel. In January 2012, that is what I began to do. Write my story, that is.

I surrounded myself with all the diaries, journaling and personal essays I had written over the years. I sat reading and reliving my past and began creating a timeline. What year did we do this? When did that happen? The timeline would have been very difficult, but with my occasional writing over the years, the who, what, when and where began to fall into place. I laughed. I cried. It was a moving, but beautiful journey.

I worked on it until November of that year. I gave a draft of the book to my best friend, Carol and my cousin, Claire and to a more recent friend, Shea, asking them to edit it for grammatical errors and to let me know if anything I'd written was unclear or confusing. The three women read it from different perspectives. Carol had shared much of what I'd lived through as it happened. Claire had been in and out of my life over the years. And since Shea knew little of my life or the people in it, her red pen notations like "who is Lorraine?" would alert me to the fact that I'd failed to fully explain who someone was when they suddenly appeared in my story. I had ended the book with my marriage to Roby. After reading what I'd written, my friends encouraged me to continue the story. So much had happened in the four years since marrying Roby . . . keep writing, they said. A part of me was disappointed; I was eager to have it complete. But I realized they were right.

I gave my friends my second draft. In the middle of December, I self-published "Permission to Shine".

The past year of writing was a blur; how it had all come together in this neat little package was a mystery. I received copies of the book just in time to give to my three sons that Christmas of 2012.

The second thing I'd always wanted to do, was perform in front of an audience . . .

∽∘∾

Karaoke

A week before my birthday, I said to Roby, "You know what my idea of a perfect birthday would be? Singing karaoke somewhere." Except for singing a song for Roby at our wedding and singing a couple songs at my cousins' birthday parties, "performing" was a relatively new venture for me. Two days later, as I opened the mail, I exclaimed to Roby,

"You are *not* going to believe this!" It was an invitation from a local non-profit organization that I had donated to. They were having a fundraiser the following Wednesday (*my birthday*) and I was invited to a fun-filled evening of karaoke. Hors d'oeuvres would be served.

For several months, I'd been downloading karaoke versions of old songs from the WWII era. I'd been practicing singing them and I didn't think I sounded half bad. Roby, ever the supportive husband, humored me and we went. I brought my own CD with the music of three songs I'd practiced. We knew no one, but everyone else seemed to know each other. Roby and I don't usually have trouble meeting and socializing with new people, but for some reason, we didn't really connect with anyone. We sat alone. When the DJ looked for volunteers, I waited and watched. Some "singers" went up in groups and were obviously just having a good time. But some of the soloists were pretty good. I finally went up (not once, but three times in the course of the evening) and got what I'd wished for. I sang on a stage, with a mic in front of an audience. The DJ gave me his card inviting me to go to another one of his gigs.

I was turning 60 and I suspected that Roby had a surprise party up his sleeve. And that it was planned for the weekend after my birthday. This I figured, when I found out the boys were coming home for a visit that weekend. The party was here at our house; Roby had ordered catered food from a great restaurant in town. My family, Roby's family and many of my friends came. It was wonderful. What I *hadn't* expected was the arrival of Lou's family from Connecticut! That Roby thought to include them *and* that they made the trip up to New Hampshire meant the world to me.

The following day, I happily relived the party. My only embarrassment was that I'd decided to entertain my guests (a captive audience) with a few songs. I guess the karaoke night went to my head.

ॐ∽⌒

The Engagement

In 2012 my youngest son presented his girlfriend with a diamond. It was not a total surprise when David and Leliah became engaged. They'd been together since David's freshman year at Babson. They had moved in together a year after college. But it was no less a delight to hear.

It is at moments like these, that I miss Lou. His son would be getting married and he wasn't here to be a part of it. He'd never met Leliah. And she'd never gotten to know David's Dad. It was a lonely feeling to realize that this joy I felt for my son could not be shared with the only other person in the world who loved him as I do . . . Lou.

This intimate love that I hold in my heart for my children, a love that only a parent can know, is something I now carry alone.

৵৽

2013

---

*"A comfort zone is a beautiful place,
but nothing ever grows there."*

– Unknown

Joyce and Mr. R.

In 2012 I had begun voice lessons with Anna, a young woman who had directed a group I'd sung with in 2011. She'd been working with me on the old 30's and 40's songs for a while. It seemed a shame not to sing them for someone. One day in January, I said to Roby,

"You know, those old songs I like to sing?"

"Yes?"

"The audience who'd enjoy them is dying away. In a few years, there won't be many people around who will even remember them!"

"That's true." Roby agreed.

"Wouldn't it be fun to go to senior centers and assisted living places and sing for them?" I continued. "We could take the speaker system and the mic and the music and put on a show."

"Hey, I'm game. I'll help you set up. I can book you at Meetinghouse for our first gig!" Meetinghouse is a senior apartments/assisted living facility where Roby had done a weekly ministry for a few years. He knew the people there.

"Really? You're willing to do that with me?" What a guy, I thought.

"Sure. Get a set together and let me know when you're ready."

It was an idea I'd been tossing around in my head for months, but hadn't pursued. I knew I only had to mention it to Roby and it would become a reality. And

I was right. For weeks he asked, "How's the music coming? Are you almost ready?"

I took my time, wanting to feel confident and prepared. I went through my songs, practicing and eliminating those I felt I didn't sing well. I looked on-line for more ideas. Finally, I chose ten that I would sing for the audience and five additional songs that we would pass out the lyrics sheets to and invite them to sing along. To break up the monotony, after my sixth song, Roby would ask to sing with me and we'd do a song together and then he'd tell a few jokes. We would call ourselves "Joyce and Mr. R."

We booked our first show in May. I prayed the audience would be forgiving. We weren't professionals! I made up a poster for "Joyce and Mr. R." that we could set up on an easel at the entrance to the room where we'd be performing. As we set up in the second-floor lounge at Meetinghouse, a woman in a wheelchair approached us.

"We'll be doing songs from the 30's and 40's," I explained.

"Oh, we had someone come in and do a sing-along with songs from the 50's'," she said. "I enjoyed *that*. I don't really care for the 30's stuff. I couldn't stand Frank Sinatra!"

As she wheeled away in the direction of the elevator, Roby and I just looked at each other.

"Well, this is a great way to start." I said. I hoped it wasn't a bad omen.

Not many chairs had been set up in the lounge. There was still a lot of empty space. I supposed that the staff didn't expect many to come. We learned that an outing to the shore had also been planned for the residents that day. Ten minutes before we were supposed to start, there were only five people. One of the ladies must have sensed my disappointment.

"Oh, don't worry," she said. "They'll come. They all show up at the last minute."

Sure enough, they began to come in. Now I understood why so few chairs had been put out. Many of the residents came in wheelchairs and filled the empty spaces. Before we knew it, there was a respectable number of people. Even the lady who hated Frank Sinatra discreetly parked herself at the back of the room.

"Where are the word sheets? Isn't this a sing-along?" A couple of people asked. Apparently, our show had been billed as a sing-along. So, I began the show by thanking them for coming and explaining that I didn't have the words for all the songs, but if they knew the words, they were welcome to sing along whenever they wanted.

It didn't take me long to realize that the reward for me was, in fact, watching their faces light up in recognition of these long-forgotten songs. Many of them were singing, some aloud, some simply mouthing the words or tapping their feet. Afterwards, they expressed their enjoyment. Some told me I had a lovely voice. And many hoped we'd come back again.

ॐॐ

Hospice Choir

Roby had been doing volunteer work with the VNA Hospice for some time. He'd gotten to know Linda, the volunteer coordinator quite well. She knew I'd sung with groups before (many years with a large woman's choral group) and told Roby to encourage me to join the Hospice choir she was hoping to get off the ground.

"Who'll be directing it?" I asked Roby when he told me about it.

"I don't think she has a director, yet," he said.

"She doesn't expect me to direct it, does she?"

"No, no, I don't think so," he said unconvincingly.

"I'm interested in joining the choir. It sounds like something I'd really enjoy. But, as a singer. I don't have any experience leading a group! Make sure Linda understands that."

In mid January, I arrived at the first meeting of the hospice choir eager to be part of this ministry. Ten interested women showed up. All of them were already Hospice Volunteers. They'd seen Linda's announcement of the newly formed choir in the Volunteer Newsletter. No one, it seemed, had any experience directing. We threw ideas around. I eagerly made a number of suggestions myself. Enough so, that I appeared to know what I was talking about. The woman to my right elbowed me. "You're it." Denise said. "What do you mean?" I whispered. "You're it . . . the director!" she said. "No, I'm *not* the director." I said. She just smiled.

By the end of the meeting, by default, I became the director. That is, (since no one else had), I reluctantly volunteered. Sue, the woman to my left must have noticed my hesitation and feeling sorry for me, volunteered to be co-director. "I have no idea what to do, but I'll help you," she said. I put forth my first directive. "For our next meeting, I'd like everyone to bring song ideas, with lyrics and CD's if you can."

After the second meeting in the board room at the VNA office, I changed the meeting place to my home. My living room was more conducive to rehearsing than a meeting room. Plus, having a piano might come in handy. In the course of the next few weeks, the task of directing seemed overwhelming. Every week presented a new challenge. Another adjustment to be made. Some of the songs I'd decided on were either too high for the altos or too low for the sopranos. I came up with harmonies. But some of the altos had never sung with a group before and singing harmony was difficult for them. They were more comfortable singing the melody. "Just sing the melody an octave lower," I compromised.

I welcomed their input and suggestions. Not only did I want them to feel that it was "our" choir, not "my" choir, but honestly, I needed all the help I could get!

Most of the members in the group were retired. Two worked full-time, but were dedicated and came to as many of the rehearsals as they could. I couldn't have asked for a more wonderful group of women. I loved each one. Any doubts I had about my ability to lead them were offset by their warm support and words of thanks for the work I put in.

When we seemed comfortable with a few songs, I recorded us singing. We cringed when we heard ourselves. We were all over the place; not in sync. I'd taught them the songs. But I hadn't directed them. I had no idea how.

"Anna, forget the singing lesson," I said to my singing teacher the following day, "Teach me how to direct!"

"What songs are you singing?" she asked.

I sang a few lines from four of our songs so that she could determine whether they were in 4/4 time or 3/4 time. She showed me how to move my hands depending on the time signature.

The following week, using the simple techniques I learned from Anna, I "directed" the choir. I continued to record our rehearsals. Later, listening to the recording, I found our singing was becoming more cohesive, but also captured on the recorder and even sweeter music to my ears was the laughter and kidding amongst the ladies between the songs. What a blessing these women were.

Meanwhile, I signed up for the 8 week Hospice Volunteer training that Linda taught. I had put the cart before the horse. A person is supposed to complete the training *before* volunteering with the VNA. But I hadn't yet sung for hospice patients. Every week I looked forward to the training class. I was learning so much about the hospice program, what to expect when visiting a hospice patient and what one can and cannot do as a volunteer.

Later that spring, we were asked by Chuck, the Hospice Chaplain, to sing at the Hospice Memorial

Service. Yearly, the VNA holds this service for families of hospice patients who have died during the year. We hadn't begun to sing for patients yet, but we were happy to have been asked to be part of this service. As we sang, we could see that the families were moved by our songs, which blessed us in return.

Rehearsals in the weeks that followed went from wonderful to horrible. I was getting burned out. I felt like I was out of my league.   I reminded Linda that I was just filling in until she could find a *real* director. "I just want to sing!" I kept telling Roby. "You're doing a great job," he always responded. "But I don't *want* to be the director!"

In July we were scheduled for our first visitation. I was apprehensive; I had no idea what to expect. Our first patient was Helen. As we began to sing at her bedside, she closed her eyes. And soon a gentle smile emerged as we continued "Morning has Broken". We asked her if she'd enjoy a couple of oldies. She perked up at the familiar melodies. The next patient was Joyce, who was younger (in her early fifties) and dying of cancer. As we sang "All Through the Night", she teared up.   When we finished our last song, Joyce was so thankful and visibly moved, as we all were by this, our first experience. The visit renewed my confidence and provided the motivation I needed to continue directing the choir.

ॐ∽ॐ

Dreams

I dreamt that I was getting ready to go out, for a ride, during a beautiful snowstorm. I was taking a long time getting ready. Preoccupied with what to wear. I knew Roby was waiting. Probably getting impatient.

"You almost ready?" It was Lou asking. And he was smiling . . . not impatient. I was surprised. Lou and Roby ... both could get impatient with my dawdling. I *am* slow. Can't blame them. But going for a ride on a snowy night? That seemed more like something Roby would do. But this time it was Lou. I wondered in the dream if I would have been happier if it had been Roby waiting for me.

I've had many dreams in which *both* men are present, and I'm usually torn between which to choose. Sometimes it's Lou. Sometimes it's Roby. No matter who I chose, I miss the other. In this dream, I was pleasantly surprised that Lou wanted to do something as romantic as taking an evening ride in a winter wonderland.

I don't tell Roby about this dream. I only tell him about the ones where he comes out the victor. He always tells me though, that when we all get to heaven, it'll be Lou that I go to, not him. Maybe he's right. But then I wonder . . . it is heaven, after all. Will I really have to chose?

ॐ◌

I owned a commercial building on Liberty Street. Once a private home, it was zoned professional space when my husband Lou bought it in 1984. A counseling center for Veterans had been the sole tenant ever since. When the Veteran's Center vacated the property last September, I decided to sell the building. Roby worked hard getting the building cleaned out and looking nice. By December we had it listed with a realtor we knew.

In March 2013 we had a buy and sell agreement with a young man named Michael. He was just beginning to buy rental property. He was so excited at the closing, I was glad he'd been the one to buy it.

A year later, Mike invited Roby and me to the building to see the changes he'd made. The interior had badly needed updating. He excitedly went from room to room, showing us the work that'd been done. Much of it with his own sweat and tears. He showed us the furniture he'd bought for the foyer. Victorian style to match the age of the house. He showed us some of the offices that had been upgraded with new paint and carpeting. Michael had the building fully occupied. He told us he had another building in the works on the West side. It was fun to see his passion and excitement. He reminded me of Lou when Lou was first starting out many years ago.

৯৶৶

On Children
by Kahlil Gibran

Your children are not your children.
They are the sons and daughters of
Life's longing for itself.
They come through you but not from you,
And though they are with you yet they belong not to you.
You may give them your love but not your thoughts,
For they have their own thoughts.
You may house their bodies but not their souls,
For their souls dwell in the house of tomorrow,
which you cannot visit, not even in your dreams.
You may strive to be like them,
but seek not to make them like you.
For life goes not backward nor tarries with yesterday.
You are the bows from which your children
as living arrows are sent forth.

Wedding Plans

My son, David and his fiancé decided their wedding would be in a vineyard in California. The wedding was set for the coming September. One trip had been made earlier to the vineyard to check it out. In March 2013, the kids were taking another trip there to make some final arrangements. Leliah's mom, Nicole would accompany them. They asked me if I'd like to go with them.

As mother of the groom, there are few opportunities to be involved in the wedding plans. I jumped at the chance to go. We landed in San Francisco and rented a car for the 3 hour drive south to Paso Robles where the wedding would be. We chose the inland route versus the coastal highway because it was much shorter. I wasn't disappointed. I was fascinated by the miles and miles of farmland. Rows and rows of red leaf lettuce stretching as far as the eye could see. Followed by romaine, tomatoes and on and on. It wasn't hard to imagine that this was where much of the produce that I bought in New Hampshire (especially in winter) probably came from. As we neared our destination, farmland turned into vineyards. We were in wine country. Winding country highways meandering past one vineyard after another. Small vineyards, with signs that invited you to free wine tastings. Further along the road, another sign, this one warning of drinking and driving!

The first day we went to the venue where David and Leliah were scheduled to meet with the wedding planner to iron out the details. It was early Spring and the vines were bare, last year's foliage and fruit long gone; but in September they would be graced with leaves and teeming with plump grapes. The kids pointed out a hill in the vineyard where the ceremony would take place and showed us the barn where dinner and the reception would be. It was a charming and romantic location. It would be a small wedding of 20 people, just immediate family and a few close friends.

Later, while David and Leliah met with the photographer, I was able to spend some time alone with Leliah's mom. It was an opportunity to get to know each other better. I enjoyed my time with Nicole. Warm and with a great sense of humor; she was fun to hang out with. And as I got to know Nicole better, the more I realized how fortunate David was to become part of this family.

The next day, Leliah and Nicole went to check out a local hair stylist. While they had their hair done, David and I took a drive to the shore. As we walked on a long pier chatting, I commented on how beautiful their engagement photos were. The pictures, taken outdoors in fields and by beautiful trees, were artistically done by a professional photographer.

"You and Roby should do that. Have some special photos taken of the two of you," David said. David had no idea what that simple comment meant to me. I had married Roby two years after my husband, David's father, died. He'd never given me reason to think otherwise, still, David's suggestion showed how supportive and accepting he was of my relationship with Roby. That meant the world to me.

The last day we checked out two restaurants that were being considered for the rehearsal dinner. The first one was a bit stuffy and formal. We'd be having a full-course formal dinner the night of the wedding; we wanted something more laid back. We found this in the second restaurant, a farm-to-table, organic place. The menu was appealing, and they had a room they could set aside just for our party. Everyone coming for the wedding would be traveling into Paso Robles that day, so the rehearsal dinner would include them all.

As our trip neared the end, I was already looking forward to coming back in September.

えへへ

Your Children

". . . You may give them your love but not your thoughts,
For they have their own thoughts.
You may house their bodies but not their souls . . . "

"Well, Mom" John said. "You're that much closer to your dream of being a grandmother."

His comment, prompted by his brother's engagement, took me by surprise. I guess I had verbalized my hope to have a grandchild more often than I'd thought. I suddenly realized that I'd been applying a subtle (or not so subtle?) pressure on my sons to fulfill my dream. It seemed less important now.

"Possibly . . .," I said to John, "But honestly, it doesn't really matter to me. It won't be the end of the world if it never happens. Of course if I had grandchildren, it would be wonderful. But what really matters to me is that you and your brothers do what is right for you. If you choose not to have children, that's okay with me."

"Wow, that is so cool that you feel that way, Mom!" John seemed surprised, impressed even.

"My only hope," I added, "is that whatever you and your partner choose, it's a mutual decision. It would be sad if one of you really wanted kids, and the other didn't."

That made sense to John. He seemed pretty sure that if he and Colette ever get to that stage in their relationship, that they would be in agreement. I assumed that would be true for David and Leliah as well. In any case, it is their decision to make, not mine.

❧❧

Asha and Sam

Asha and Sam had been living at my apartment building for two years. They were now engaged to be married. Asha asked if it would be okay for her parents to stay at the apartment the weekend of the wedding. When I gave my approval, she went on to ask about the empty apartment on the second floor. "I'll have a lot of family coming from out of town. Would it be all right if some of them used the empty apartment for the weekend?"

Asha and Sam were a delightful couple and always respectful. I didn't hesitate to say yes. "My parents don't know that we are living together. So Sam will be with a friend that weekend," she added.

Asha was Indian and I thought perhaps her family was coming from India, but they lived in the U.S., she said. Some of her relatives were coming from Canada. Sam's family was coming from New York. A few days before the wedding, Roby and I went to give them the key to the empty apartment and also brought a small gift.

"Would it be alright if my cousins decorate the empty apartment for a pre-wedding ceremony that is a tradition in our culture?" Asha asked.

"Of course," we said.

"And I would really like you both to come to the ceremony," she said.

"Are you sure? Wouldn't we be intruding?" I asked.

"Oh no! Not at all. I would really love for you to come!"

Roby and I looked at each other. We were surprised and honored.

"Yes, we'd love to!"

The ceremony was the night before the wedding. We got there early. Asha's female cousins were busily going from Asha's apartment on the third floor to the one below. They looked absolutely lovely in their colorful sari's and jewelry. They were excited to show us the apartment. Roby and I looked in awe. We hardly recognized it. It had been beautifully transformed. Colorful orange fabric edged with paisley designs and silky white fabric had been draped over the living room window. Tall palm plants with strands of lit white lights, sat on either side. A jute rug for sitting was placed between them with pots of white flowers at its front corners. A sheet was spread over the living room carpet and covered futon mattresses lined each of the two long walls. The living room opened up to the kitchen where a long table had been placed against the wall, set up for a buffet style meal after the ceremony.

When the time of the ceremony drew near, the female cousins stood in the hallway "waiting." One of Asha's young male cousins was kind enough to explain what would take place.

"When Sam and his family arrive, they will be greeted outside the apartment door by the young women. One of them has a box of chocolates and will offer one to each guest; another of the women will hand each one a rose; another a small gift. It is a show of respect and welcome. Sam will enter after the rest of his family."

When Sam and his family finally arrived, it felt like a surprise party.

"They're here, they're here. Get ready!" the girls whispered to one another.

Roby and I stood in the stairway watching. I asked the male cousin if it would be improper to take some pictures. "Not at all," he said. In fact, we would later see a number of these young adults raising their cell phones to snap photos of the ceremony.

After the welcome of the groom's family, Roby and I were motioned to go in. We were joined by the cousins. A pile of shoes at the doorway indicated that we were to remove our shoes.

"No, you don't have to," said one of the cousins.

The shoes had been removed by the groom's family who sat on the futon cushions along the wall and on the covered carpet in the center. The rest of us stood by the far wall or sat on the uncovered carpet. We sat waiting, not really sure what it was we were waiting for.

Then some of Asha's older relatives entered. Aunts and Uncles. Two of the men stood apart from each other and held a red sheer fabric up high forming a canopy at the doorway under which Asha entered. She looked lovely in a colorful traditional Indian dress of orange and red, beaded jewelry on her head and arms. Her hands were beautifully painted with henna designs. I would learn later that henna, also known as Mehndi is a paste associated with positive spirits and good luck. The Mehndi ceremony, held the night before the wedding is carried out by the women in the family as a way of wishing the bride good health and prosperity.

Asha joined Sam sitting on the jute rug and the ceremony began. On the floor before the couple sat a bowl of fruit, Indian sweets and a bowl containing a yellow paste made of turmeric, oil and water. Beginning with the groom's parents, each guest, one by one, knelt by the couple, offering them a bite of food, then dipped their finger in the paste and put a dab on the bride and groom's faces. The ritual symbolized a wish for good luck to the soon to be married couple.

After Sam's family, the bride's side followed, beginning with Asha's father. And then the apartment door opened. In came Asha's mother with an aunt who'd gone to get her. The woman never looked up as she briskly made her way to the bride and groom, hurriedly did what was expected and stormed back out.

Roby and I looked at each other with raised eyebrows. Was Asha's mother not feeling well? Is that why she hurried?

There was an air of tension in the room. Asha looked clearly shaken. The rest of her family carried on with the ceremony; her aunts and uncles and cousins. The aunt who had brought her mother down returned and took part, smiling at Asha, trying to lighten up the mood.

I wasn't certain if Roby and I could participate, but her family invited us to take our turn. I went first and then Roby. Afterwards the bride and groom remained seated while the others began to mingle. Asha motioned me to come to her.

"I'm so glad you came," she said when I knelt by her. "You probably noticed something was wrong."

"What is it? Is your mother ill?" I asked.

"No. She will not accept that I am marrying someone who is not Indian. I am the first in our family to do so. She is very angry about it."

"I'm so sorry, Asha."

"It's very hurtful."

"Maybe when she gets to know Sam. He's a wonderful man." I tried to offer hope.

"She has met him many times. I hoped when we got engaged, she would change her mind about him. But to marry outside our culture is unthinkable to her."

I felt deeply sad for Asha and Sam. But as I looked around at Asha's family, the young, the old, the single, the married . . . *all* Indian, I couldn't help but get a sense of what the old woman must be feeling. In her eyes, the thread of this family, rich in a tradition and culture going back thousands of years, had been broken. Could it be that Asha's marrying outside this tradition was an insult to something deeply ingrained in the woman's sense of who she is and who she had hoped Asha was? Maybe one day her mother will come to understand that her non-acceptance of Asha's husband will tear the fabric of the family apart more than Asha's decision.

కురిం

The Wedding

In September Roby, my son Michael and I headed to California to join up with the others for the wedding. Roby had never been to the west coast. We spent a couple nights in San Francisco before heading to Paso Robles. Michael had a chance to spend some time with friends who lived in San Francisco. From there we headed to Paso, taking our time and enjoying some sightseeing on the way.

Roby, honored to have been asked, would officiate the wedding. He joined the wedding party on Friday night for the rehearsal, followed by the rehearsal dinner when everyone came together.

Saturday was a beautiful day for the wedding. It literally never rains in Paso this time of year. So it was a great surprise to everyone when rain clouds made an appearance shortly before the ceremony was to begin, causing a short delay. The shower ended as quickly as it had appeared, but the photographer was able to take advantage of the ensuing misty fog rolling through the vineyard hills which made for some stunning wedding photos.

David's brothers were his best men; Leliah's sister her maid of honor. Slowly they made their way up the hill as the guests waited at the top. Leliah was accompanied by her parents. It was a beautiful ceremony highlighted by the vows David and Leliah made to each other, which were thoughtful, heartfelt and exquisitely written. The wedding was followed by a reception in the barn . . .

dinner and dancing. Leliah and her father danced to "Unforgettable" by Nat King Cole; David had chosen "What a Wonderful World" by Louis Armstrong for our dance together.

The festivities continued the following afternoon back at the vineyard, where David and Leliah had planned outdoor competition -- pitting "David's Team" against "Leliah's Team", complete with t-shirts bearing our team names. Playing games that included balancing a marble on a ruler, being the first to unfurl a roll of crepe paper or flipping an Oreo from your forehead into your mouth (with hands behind your back), none of us escaped making a fool of ourselves.

Later that afternoon we boarded a chartered bus that took us to the shore for a picnic and campfire on the beach. The sunset over the Pacific was a beautiful way to end what had been an awesome weekend.

ॐॐ

"A wise tribal elder told a story to his grandson
one evening by the fire.

'Inside me, there is
a fight raging between two wolves.
One wolf is fear, anger, self-pity, envy,
greed, arrogance and sorrow.
The other wolf is love, faith, hope, peace,
forgiveness, humility, kindness and joy.
Both wolves are strong, and they battle fiercely –
not just in me, but in everyone, even you.'

The young boy thought for a moment and asked,
'Grandfather, which wolf will win?'

The wise elder replied, 'The one you feed.'"

-- Cherokee proverb

David and Leliah live in a condominium in Jersey City . . . five hours from us.   Leliah's family is less than two hours from them. Her dad Don is there when they need someone to teach them how to prep a wall before painting, or cut tiles for the bathroom floor.

David was in college when Roby and I got married. He has never lived at home since Roby and I have been together. The bond between them is growing, but living so far away doesn't afford Roby those opportunities to play a bigger role in David's life. And to be able, like Don, to share his knowledge and experience with David, teaching and helping him with the projects that come with home ownership.

With his own father gone, and Roby not close by, I'm comforted that David has a father in Don. With only daughters, I'm sure that Don enjoys having a "son". David has been embraced by and is dearly loved by everyone in Leliah's family.   For that, I'm thankful.

ॐॐ

The Lady at the Checkout

I greeted her warmly. The bagger at the checkout. I used to try to avoid her. She is an older woman, who moves slower than molasses and if you tried to help her, she would give you a look that said "What's the matter, I'm not doing it good enough??"

But these days, I seek her out. Most people her age would be retired, but she works. I smile and say good morning. She says good morning back and I can tell she appreciates the acknowledgement. "Do you mind if I help?" I ask with a smile. "No, I don't mind," she smiles back.

We all need a little understanding.

ৡৄ

The Robe

While I seek to act, think and speak from a place of love and not from my ego, I often fail. Usually I'm aware when I do. And awareness is the beginning.

Selfishness, being judgmental, our ego . . . they are all part of our human condition. Moving beyond this conditioned behavior is not only possible but necessary to align ourselves with our spiritual center. The lessons are there in our lives, every day: in our dealings with other people, in our spiritual readings, in the consequences of the decisions we make, and in the words and actions of those who embody the attributes we aspire to.

The latter being the case when my brother and wife visited last year. Judy and Al were still "newlyweds", married the year after Roby and I. I enjoyed our time with them and getting to know Judy. I fell in love with her. She is sweet, kind and fun to be with. Each morning when Judy came down for coffee, I told her how much I loved her nightgown and robe. They were a matching set made of lightweight flannel in an adorable blue and white pattern. "Al says it reminds him of Wedgewood china," Judy laughed.

When Roby and I returned home from bringing Al and Judy to the airport I found the nightgown and robe neatly folded on the chair in the guestroom. A note lay on them from Judy. She wanted me to have them. She knew how much I loved them and so she left them for me.

I was embarrassed, somewhat, that I had expressed so passionately how much I like them. How could Judy have parted with them so easily? How was it possible to be so unselfish? I know I could not have been so generous.

Months later I would come to realize that Judy had left me so much more than a gown and robe. I was showing a visiting friend a photo I'd had enlarged and matted. "I love it," she said. "Can you make me a copy?" I was about to say, that yes, I could make a copy and mail it to her. (I had, after all, gone to the trouble of enlarging and matting this one it for myself). Then I thought of Judy. Instead I said, "Here, take this one."

Often now, when in a situation where I could easily take the selfish route, I think of "Judy and the robe" and choose instead to put the other person first.

What Judy left me was a desire to cultivate a generous spirit like her own.

৯৵৶

Nia

She is a Saudi woman and a graduate student at a university here. She rents an apartment from me. Nia wears the traditional head covering whenever she is out. But I've seen her without it in the privacy of her apartment. "I wish you could see her without it. Her hair is beautiful," I tell Roby. Nia will not allow a man to see her without her head covered. Covered or not, she is lovely, her smile especially beautiful.

I introduced Nia to Sharon, the tenant across the hall from her. Sharon is in her 50's and on disability, so she's home mostly. She readily befriended Nia. Nia is lonely here in the States. For a Saudi woman to travel so far without a companion is not acceptable in her culture. Her brother's plans to accompany her fell through. She came over with her father, who comes back every few months to check on her. Even here, Nia will usually find another woman to go places with. In Sharon, she has found someone to sit and talk to. Sharon is a compassionate and friendly woman who is also a great listener. Nia shares pictures with Sharon, telling her about her family. She tells Sharon how badly some of the teachers treat her and other Middle-Eastern women, especially those who remain true to their religion wearing the hijab to cover their heads. Since 9-11, people of her ethnicity are often looked upon with suspicion. Nia is a deeply religious, spiritual woman. But because of religious extremists, the Muslim faith is misunderstood. She will graduate soon and has no desire to remain here; she's eager to go back home.

Nia tells me that the way American women dress and behave is disturbing to her . . . understandable, given her way of life. It's not hard to see what Nia sees in some of the college girls. . . women scantily dressed, a seeming lack of moral discipline, values so different from her own.

But I believe that there is a core of decency within most people. Lack of understanding of one another's cultures can cause us all to be judgmental.

৯৹৶৩

Making Friends with My Voice

While there are many songs that I sing with confidence and comfort, there are still songs (in our Joyce and Mr. R. repertoire) that I feel ill-equipped to sing. I still lack confidence in my head voice (falsetto). I have convinced myself that I cannot sing many of the slower songs well. And as I keep telling myself this, I continue to believe I can't improve. Even though Anna has told me that some of these songs suit my range and that I do, in fact, sing them well, I feel insecure about them.

Recently I listened more closely to the voices of some famous artists, some old, some current. They don't all possess classically rich and fluid voices. Some, like Rod Stewart, for example, have a raspy voice. But their voices are unique to them and I enjoy their songs.

I realize that I have to tell myself a different story. That my voice is unique to me. It's neither "good" nor "bad". It's *mine*. And I need to embrace my uniqueness. If I put myself into my songs and convey feeling behind the words, then the audience will enjoy listening. They will feel it too . . . and that's what matters.

❧❧

NAMI

Roby and I attend the NAMI (National Alliance for Mental Illness) support groups regularly. I'd first become involved when a loved one was diagnosed with mental illness eight years ago. He manages his illness well and is emotionally in a good place now. But we continue to attend the meetings to support others whose journey with their loved one's illness is currently difficult.

Someone at last night's meeting spoke of panic attacks. I was surprised to find myself discussing my own battle with panic attacks when I was in my 20's. I even revealed my breakdown at age 12 and the subsequent social anxiety I experienced in high school. I rarely speak of that time in my life. And until last night I'd never thought much about the connection between my experience and mental illness. Those at the meeting found it remarkable that I had never spoken of my panic attacks to anyone, let alone sought any help, and yet somehow I'd learned how to deal with it.

On the way home I felt uneasy. I wished I hadn't said anything. I felt vulnerable. I feared that just thinking of panic attacks would bring them back. Not wishing to let my fears escalate, I remembered a lesson I'd learned from Pema Chodron, a Buddhist nun whose books I've benefited greatly from. She speaks of training our minds. When emotions arise in us that do not serve our well-being or those around us (like anger, jealousy, fear, etc.), Pema tells us to not feed the fire. To acknowledge the feeling and allow yourself to feel it. But don't let your mind tell you stories that will cause the emotions to escalate.

For example, if there is a person in your life who invariably causes you to be angry, simply acknowledge the feeling but don't allow the "stories" in your mind to fuel the anger. The story may be, "This person thinks she is smarter or better than I am." or "This person goes out of his way to be mean to me." or "I wish I knew why she hates me so much!" The fact is . . . we have no idea what fuels another's behavior. Does he *really* think he is smarter than you are? Or is it possible he feels insecure and it is his way of protecting himself? Does she intentionally seek to be mean? Or are there factors in her life that have made her a bitter person? Does he really hate you? We fill our minds with stories all the time. We expect things *are* as we perceive them. When they seldom are. The healthier response would be to acknowledge our emotion and then let it go.

That night, I allowed myself to feel uncomfortable. Then I released the belief that these feelings would cause the panic attacks to return.

ॐॐ

It had been two years since I'd written "Raising Well-Behaved Kids . . . a simple guide." The impetus for creating the book came from my observation that many parents seem to lack an understanding of the importance of discipline. I asked myself, "If someone were to ask my advice on parenting, what would I tell them?" I began writing. *"What is Discipline? Discipline is teaching a child what is acceptable behavior and what isn't. And, teaching a child that there are consequences when he/she does not behave in an acceptable manner."* It seems too many parents believe they should be their child's "friend", not their teacher. In fact, children not only *need* rules and guidance, deep down they *want* them. Having guidelines and knowing what is expected of them, gives children a sense of stability. I continued to write . . . about following through, manners and respect, honesty, setting a good example, disciplining with love, to name a few.

Before I knew it, a book was taking shape; a book that I wanted to share. I created a short, easy to read book with the hope that even those who are not proficient readers, or don't have time to read a lengthy book, would pick this book up and read it. In 2012, I self-published it, had 30 copies printed and began to approach non-profits whose programs serve young parents through education, counseling, day care or other services. If they were interested, I would provide the books for free . . . as many copies as they wanted.

The books were well-received. I was now distributing them to several organizations. Mostly the books were simply made available for parents to take. I provide display boxes for the books, that say "*Free-Take One.*"

In the summer of 2014, I received an e-mail from a non-profit organization in Concord that serviced young parents, both with day-care services and as a resource center. "We've developed a six-week parenting course based on your book. We would like you to come to our last class so that the parents can meet you."

I had hoped that the book would also be used as an educational tool. And while this was not the first place that had expressed an interest in doing so, as far as I knew, this was the first time that one of them had developed a course specifically based on the book. I was excited.

A week later I received a Thank You note from a Family Resource center in Derry, for all the books I had given to their organization. Another note was enclosed asking if I would consider being a guest speaker at one of their parenting support groups, or even do a parenting workshop.

The thought was overwhelming. Though I'd had no trouble pointing out the things I felt were important when raising children in my book, I hardly felt qualified to speak on the subject. Roby thought otherwise. I resisted, but the next day I was sitting at my computer writing ideas for a possible presentation. I knew that if I took the time, I could prepare something worthwhile and would feel comfortable speaking. But I had to ask myself if this was something I really wanted to do. There were so many other things that I was currently putting my energy into. I felt it would be unwise to commit to doing something unless I could devote the time to do it right. I told the director as much and declined, thanking her and letting her know how pleased I was to have been asked.

(In 2018 I edited the book and republished it under the name "Raising Great Kids".)

ॐॐ

The Bad Dream

In the middle of the night I awake from a bad dream. I dreamt that I'd seen my son driving down a road, then pull over. A man in a truck behind him pulled over as well, and got out of his vehicle and began to yell at him in anger and began to punch him. Maybe he had cut the man off by mistake. Whatever the reason, it hadn't warranted such an angry reaction. As the man drove off, I wanted to track him down. I was so mad. I wanted to scream, "What is the matter with you? Do you really think that he did it on purpose just to anger you? Seriously? Can't you give a guy a break? You mean to say you never make a mistake?"

I awake with a heavy heart. Why are there so many angry people? People who can't see beyond their own little world and their own needs. I want to protect my son from an angry world. I lay awake for a long time, unable to shake the feelings of anger and sadness. Troubled with the state of this world. If this is God's world and He's in control why doesn't He intervene? My thoughts go round and round. It seems as though sleep will never come.

Then I think about the story of Jesus. As a human on this earth he had been an innocent gentle soul. He meant no one harm. Indeed, he loved everyone. And yet he had been persecuted and ridiculed. And they killed him. But as he hung on the cross he said "Father, forgive them for they know not what they do."

I think again about the man in the dream. I can't begin to know what causes people like him to be so unhappy and bitter. But I know that being angry back serves no purpose other than to shake the peace in my own heart. I forgive him. Now I only feel sorrow for the many wounded people this man represents. People who don't know how to love or accept Love.

And I release the need to protect my son; I know that his own inner strength will sustain him.

. . . finally, sleep comes.

෯෴෯

Claudia

In the summer of 2014 we would have the pleasure of hosting the mom of my son John's partner, Colette. Claudia is from Berlin, Germany. For many years when Colette and her sister were growing up, the family lived in Florida. With ties to the States, Claudia, a teacher, often uses her summer vacation time to come to the States to visit friends in Florida and then to NYC to visit with close friends and of course, Colette and John.

We'd met Claudia a couple years earlier in New York City. Roby and I had taken an immediate liking to her and we were delighted when she expressed an interest in visiting us. She'd never been to New Hampshire and she wanted to see where John grew up.

Her visit overlapped briefly with my yearly summer visit from my friend, Gabe. Though Gabe was born in the States and grew up here in New Hampshire, her family is German. Her parents have died; the only family she has left are all in Germany and she hardly knows them. I hadn't heard Gabe speak German since her mom died years earlier. So, it was fun to hear Gabe and Claudia carry on a conversation in German, oblivious to Roby and I who understood nothing. "They could be talking about us, for all we know!" I said to Roby.

Claudia was the perfect guest. I had worried about how we could entertain a woman who had traveled all over the world. What would possibly interest her? But the answer to that was easy, "everything".

Claudia loved history and was eager to visit Manchester's historical museum. She read with interest about Manchester's Amoskeag Manufacturing Company and how it grew to be the largest cotton textile mill in the world. She was drawn to the sector that spoke of Manchester's early German population and its neighborhood on the City's west side.

She enjoyed the simplicity of an afternoon at a nearby park, listening to an oldies rock and roll band play on the bandstand. Along with lawn chairs, Roby and I brought cheese and crackers and wine. Michael met up with us too, and before long, Claudia had us all up dancing.

One day, we went to the Currier Museum of Art. Another, we drove up to Lake Winnipesaukee so Claudia could see the area that John spoke so fondly of when reminiscing about his childhood and the times spent at the lake. Those times always included a trip to the Olde Country store in Moultonboro; I had to bring Claudia there. The store boasts a vast array of unique items; including candies from my childhood: candy cigarettes and sugar dots on strips of paper. Amongst the wares, stood a player piano waiting for someone to bring it to life.. I put a quarter in and keys of the piano began to move. The music played and Claudia began to dance, taking my hands to join her.

I was struck by Claudia's curiosity about the places she's visiting and by her pure enjoyment of life. I imagine that wherever her travels take her, Claudia embraces the experience with enthusiasm and a childlike wonder.

What a wonderful way to be.

෨෩

The Vision Board

Months after Lou died, I'd created a "Vision Board." On a peg board I pinned pictures that depicted the things I envisioned for myself. I had pinned various clipart pictures which included a meditating Buddha which represented my desire to grow spiritually; a book (on which I'd typed the title: "Only the Heart Knows") representing the book I hoped to someday write; a man and woman holding hands -- a hope for future love; a picture of lush flower beds, signifying an expansion of my perennial garden. I'd pinned a photo of my apartment building with a "full" sign photo-shopped in front of it. I'd cut out a picture of a thin woman from an L.L. Bean catalogue with a photo of my face replacing that of the model. And lastly, I'd pinned the word "SIMPLIFY".

Recently I came across the Vision Board tucked in the closet of one of the guest bedrooms. Eight years later, much of what I had seen for myself has come to pass. I'm in a better place spiritually; I've written my memoir (not the novel I'd hoped, but a book, none-the-less); I'm at a comfortable weight; I fell in love with Roby and together we've expanded the gardens. The apartment building is not currently full. But we always find a new tenant when one vacates. As far as "Simplify" . . . well, I still need to work on that one!

I wonder . . . if I made a new Vision Board . . . what would it look like?

సౌ≪

The Walkway

With plans to re-stain the house, it seemed a fitting time to repaint the shutters and doors new colors. After 30 plus years, it was time for a facelift! (For the house, not me.)

With the house freshly painted, I looked at the front steps and walkway and noticed for the first time, just how awful they looked! The concrete was blackened and cracked. The stairs had settled years ago creating quite a drop down to the top landing from the front door. Roby had added a wooden step to make up for it.

"I would love a stone walkway . . . brown stones . . . and a gentle curve to give the walkway more character." I told Roby. With this vision, we found ourselves in the showroom of a local stone and masonry contractor. There we met another customer, a man who did landscaping and walkways who was browsing the stone options for a client. He gave us his card and we called him the next day. Paul came to the house and after explaining to him what we wanted, he walked around the yard and into the back taking note of the stone patio and stepping stone paths that led from one garden to another. He invited us to come to his place of business the following Saturday.

A sign marked the entrance to a dirt road that led to a clearing on the woodsy property where he kept his equipment and worked with granite. Granite was Paul's specialty. His passion. He'd built a machine that could cut a boulder of granite into neat "slices" three inches thick.   These he used to make walkways, patios, stepping stones etc. He could transform granite into beautiful birdbaths, lampposts, tables, chairs and fountains.

I'd been looking for a new birdbath for the last two years. The one I had was plastic. I wanted something natural. I'd seen many ceramic ones. But none spoke to me.   When Roby and I caught sight of the stone birdbaths, it was not a matter of "should we", but "which one"?   We were both drawn to the same one.   That decision was easy; whether to commission Paul to do our stairs and walk . . . I needed to think about. While he would use stones of my preference, he tried to convince me that the granite would look beautiful.

"I'll think about it."

I couldn't help thinking that Paul had an agenda. He cut his own granite; of course he'd like me to choose his stones.

The next day I decided to go with Paul. His childlike excitement about his work impressed me.   He had another job to finish, and said he'd call us when he was ready.   A few weeks later he called to say he had completed the granite steps. He couldn't wait for us to see them. Paul knew I preferred a darker shade than the gray that most granite stairs were made of.

"Those must be our stairs." Roby spotted them near Paul's machinery. The stone was a darker gray with brown speckles.

"What do you think?" Paul said as he approached us.

"They're beautiful!" we both said.

"I've never made a set of stairs with this color granite," he said, " I thought you'd like it."

Then we spoke about the sidewalk. He pointed to some stones he thought would be nice.

"These are cut from three different rocks. That'll give it some variation."

"They don't look dark enough." I said.

He took a cup of water and poured it on a granite slab. "Look. See how beautiful the granite is when wet?" The color deepened to a lovely shade of brown.

"Yes, but it won't always be wet!" I said.

"Give it a coat of linseed oil and it will look just like it does when it's wet."

"Okay." I said hesitantly.

"I know you wanted smaller size stones, but this is a walk, not a garden path. I know what you like from seeing your yard. But larger ones would really be more suitable. And the stone will blend in with the theme you have going."

"But, I really wanted . . . "

"Open your mind. See the possibilities."

"I have an open mind."

He raised an eyebrow and half-smiled, as if to say, "Are you sure?"

Now I didn't have the dark brown stones I'd originally envisioned OR the size I wanted. What Paul said made sense and I reluctantly agreed. But, it was beginning to feel like Paul's walkway, not mine.

We watched as the project progressed. The stairs looked wonderful. And the walk was taking shape.

"I don't see much of a curve." I said when more than half the stones had been laid.

"It has to be a very slight curve. We have to work within the parameters we have." Paul said.

We were gone the day that Paul completed the job. When we returned I looked at the walk and could only think how different it was from what I had wanted.

"What's wrong? You look upset." Roby asked the next morning.

"The sidewalk! It's not my sidewalk, it's Paul's! I wanted dark brown stones. I went along with the granite. I wanted smaller stones. Paul insisted they had to be large. I was at least holding out for a curve! It's barely noticeable!"

Roby let me rant on without saying a word. He didn't defend Paul's work or point out the obvious --- it still was a beautiful walk.

"I know what's going to happen," I thought to myself. "By the time I see Paul, I'll no longer be angry and I'll probably have fallen in love with *his* sidewalk! I don't want that to happen!" Or so I told myself. But deep down I hoped that was true.

The next day Roby oiled the stones as Paul had instructed. The variations and the rich color in the stones came to life. When Paul came by the following day I was glad I'd gotten past my childish tirade.

"I know you wanted more of a curve, but I had to work within the area between the irrigation lines. And you'll notice I cut some of the bigger rocks to give the walk a nice balance of larger and smaller stones."

He really had worked hard to please me. I was relieved that he hadn't stopped by two days earlier, when my words would have been unjustly critical. I admired the walk.

"I *do* love it. It's beautiful." I looked at him.

He just looked at me.

"Hey, I came around," I said.

"But it wasn't easy," Paul said. I looked at him with an expression that challenged his words.

"It took time. Change is hard for you."

His words stung. Was he right? Was I really that inflexible? That night I thought about his words. I pride myself on being able to accept and adapt to things I have no control over. But it is also true, that when I make up my mind about something, I resist a change in plans. It is difficult for me to change my mind if someone is trying to persuade me in a different direction than I intended even if what the other person is suggesting makes sense. It is *my* vision after all, and I still have a choice. If I relinquish that choice with any measure of doubt, I tend to berate myself for giving in. Eventually I adapt.

Perhaps the problem is not in adapting to change, but realizing when it is time to let go, and trust. When I chose Paul to do the job, there was an unspoken agreement. I was saying, "I trust you. I have faith in your ability and expertise." Paul was saying, "I will give you something you will love and be proud of." Paul lived up to his side of the agreement. I hadn't.

Weeks later I stumbled on something that made me laugh. "Look," I said to Roby. I showed him a magazine article I found tucked in the pocket of my garden binder. I'd torn it out of a garden magazine in 2003 (eleven years ago)! It showed step-by-step instructions for a stone walkway. The picture of the finished walkway looked incredibly like the one Paul had created.

"Paul *did* know what I wanted!"

চ৵৵

Ray

I would not even mention Ray, or his memorial service if it were not for words spoken, not once, but again and again. Words describing Ray. I'd never spoken to Ray. He was a member at our church. When Roby told me he'd died, I couldn't even put a face to the name. Not until I saw a picture of him with his obituary. I remember seeing him on Sundays. He was unassuming. Quiet. I'd heard he had cancer. I thought he'd beaten it. But next I knew there was talk of him being at the hospice house.

At the funeral, a number of people went up to speak about him, what he'd meant to them, how he'd affected their lives. Family members, church friends, young men who Ray had mentored in youth group years earlier. Some spoke of Ray's offers to help them with electrical jobs (he was an electrician) even when the cancer had progressed and he seemed to be struggling. He never complained when in pain. He never said, "Why me?"

The stories varied, but one common thread came through from each person who'd known Ray. That Ray never spoke ill of anyone. Ever. He was uncomfortable when others did so, leaving the room rather than participate or listen. There are few people who that could be said of.

It's something to think about . . . certainly a virtue to aspire to.

⮞⮜

Special Occasion

Every now and then someone forwards me a thought provoking e-mail. This was one of them:

A man opened his wife's underwear drawer and picked up a silk paper wrapped package. He unwrapped the box and stared at both the silk paper and the box.

"She got this the first time we went to New York, eight or nine years ago. She has never put it on. She was saving it for a special occasion. Well, I guess this is it," he said. He got near the bed and placed the gift box next to the other clothing he was taking to the funeral home. His wife had just died.

He turned to his friend and said: "Never save something for a special occasion. Every day in your life is a special occasion."

I had learned this lesson soon after Roby and I married.   He was setting the table as I was preparing dinner. From a cupboard at the far end of the kitchen he pulled down a lovely oval shaped depression platter that once was my mother's.

"What is that for?" I asked him.

"For the asparagus," he said.

I'd only used the platter for special occasions.   In other words: hardly ever.

I looked at Roby as he placed it on the counter matter-of-factly and I thought, "Of course, we should use it. Why not?"

❧❧

Monty

He didn't always have a name. But when a week had passed and the little frog continued to come to our small garden pond, I named him Monty. Silly, I guess, but I'd always wanted a frog to live in my pond. The idea of importing one from the campground where we used to go every summer entered my mind, but there were no guarantees it would stay. Besides, it seemed cruel to remove an animal from his home. So when Monty appeared one day, I delighted in his presence, but thought surely he'd be gone the next day. As each day passed I grew more hopeful that he would call this home.

Weeks went by and we watched Monty grow. He was not bothered by the squirrels and chipmunks who came to drink at the pond or the birds who came to bathe. It's mid October now and the nights are getting cold. Frogs instinctively find a place to hole themselves up for the winter. (Not in water, as they need to breathe). There is a heater in the pond to prevent it from freezing and I'm concerned that Monty will be confused and not do what he needs to do to protect himself from the elements. Perhaps he thinks he's hit pay dirt; lucky to have ended up in a "hot spring" that will keep him warm all winter. But if he remains active, what will he eat? Roby wants to buy frog food. I'm not sure we should interfere.

Whether or not Monty makes it through the winter and delights us again next spring, I'm happy for the time we were able to enjoy his company.

స్త్రా

Roby and I have entertained at a number of senior living places as "Joyce and Mr. R." Today, we weren't sure what to expect. We'd been asked to come and perform at the Easter Seals center. We hadn't known the scope of their senior program and hadn't expected many people. But we were pleasantly surprised to find the room fill up with more than forty eager seniors by the time we began. They proved to be an enthusiastic group.

I enjoy the smiles and interaction with every group we sing for. At each show, there are often two or three with whom I feel a connection. Making eye contact with the audience as I sing, some people appear embarrassed and avert their eyes; others readily return my smile. And there are those whose response is incredibly supportive and encouraging. Just as the preacher, who hopes his message is reaching someone in the pews is buoyed by an enthusiastic "Amen" from one of them, so am I lifted by the smiling person who looks at me with a "thumbs up" expression that seems to say, "Keep going. You're doin' great!" Today I get that affirmation from many of them.

I realize in a deeper sense than I had before, that performing is a two way street. You are giving something, and as each person is receiving it in their own way, you get something back. It's an awesome feeling.

☙❧

Concern with Detail

Not to be confused with OCD, a very real and debilitating condition, I suspect we all have varying degrees of obsession with detail. Mine manifests itself in different areas of my life. Towels must be folded with the tag inside. When I make my bed in the morning, I swiftly walk back and forth from one side to the other adjusting the bedspread until it hangs equally on each side. "Would you like a measuring tape?" Roby will ask. (He has learned that even when he helps me make the bed, I always check his side.)

The same can be said for filling the dishwasher. Roby often fills it, knowing perhaps that I will rearrange it anyway. Glasses on the outside edge of the top rack, leaving the middle for small plates and little bowls. Bottom rack: all plates in a row, shortest in front to tallest in back. Bowls on opposite side - same rules. Utensils not too crowded, sharp knives in the last section. Even items *I've* put in earlier in the day will be rearranged to accommodate items added later, so as not to disrupt the proper flow. Michael's friend calls this dishwasher Tetris.

When I start a new project, be it business, music, art etc, a fair amount of time is spent getting organized before I begin. And it usually involves a binder that *must* have the proper cover, computer generated with just the right font and appropriate graphic art, which, thanks to the free clip art on Google, I can easily spend a half hour scouring through hundreds of pictures before finding the perfect one!

Most pathetic is my obsession with selecting just the right bookmark before I start a new book. I do have a favorite one for novels, but if I can't find it, I reach for my envelope of bookmarks. (It took me a while to find just the right envelope to keep them in, by the way.) I have this thing about making bookmarks. I've made some with quotes, which, of course required finding just the right picture to go with them (thank you, Google). Bookmarks for cookbooks. Inspirational bookmarks using some of my garden photos. I print them on linen cover stock; I love the texture. I see the potential for bookmarks in greeting cards I receive. After the cards have been displayed for a respectable amount of time, the paper cutter will eliminate the text and reduce the lovely artwork on the card to the appropriate size for a bookmark. Giving a book as a gift? That requires a matching bookmark, of course!

"Making bookmarks, again?" Roby will take note. It's his fault, really. When he moved in, he brought along this wonderful laminating machine. If ever I'm laminating something that doesn't take up the whole sheet, and there is room to squeeze in a bookmark or two, I'll create some so as not to waste a perfectly good laminating pouch!

❧❦

The Old Dresser Drawer

Roby and I decided to re-do the master bedroom. The furniture was dark and bulky. It was already old when Lou and I bought the set at an estate sale when we got married and moved into this house over thirty-five years ago. For a long time I have wanted something simple in a light wood. We decided on Amish furniture. It would be weeks before the furniture came in. Plenty of time to clean out the old dresser drawer.

The top drawer of this thousand year old bureau is only four inches from top to bottom. But it is over four feet wide (the width of the bureau) and deep. So deep, I'm convinced there is no back wall. Over the years, various things have been tossed in this drawer and there is always something or other that needs to be moved or pressed down in order to close it again. For as long as I can remember, every time I've opened it to get something, I've thought "I really should clean out this drawer".

Somehow it could never be done. How do you clean out a drawer full of memories? It looks like a junk drawer; in fact it is a "treasure" drawer. In the process of looking for whatever it is I need, I never fail to pull out a memory. I savor it for a moment, put it back and say to myself, "I really need to clean out this drawer!" Well, of necessity, that time had come. Taking my time, I took out each item, reliving the memory it held . . .

- a little wooden plaque with a picture and bible verse, made by and given to me by my brother Al almost 20 years ago. (At least I thought he gave it to me until I recently noticed my sister Donna's name on the back.)

-my growth charts from each pregnancy

-a packing list for the hospital when the baby comes ...I'll never need that again!

-scraps of paper with entries charting my attempts at weight loss after each birth...some with successful results; others thrown into the drawer in disgust when the pounds didn't come off.

-baggies with baby teeth left under my boys' pillows. I don't know whose teeth they are. Either John's or David's; Michael never did surrender his teeth to the tooth fairy.

-"I love you, Mom" notes

-9 volt batteries

-yellow highlighter

-scotch tape

(as if I ever remembered these things were there when I needed them)

-old eye glasses

-comb

-floss

-heart shape soap put in the drawer for its fragrance (which wore out back in 1985)

-pencils with broken tips (did I think they would miraculously sharpen themselves?)

-travel sewing kit

-pin cushion with no pins

-special cards from Lou

-an attachment to a hair dryer I no longer have

-a broken flashlight (waiting for the same miracle as
the pencils)
-cub scout belt loop
-a key (to who knows what)
-a book on yoga
-page from a magazine with tearjerker poems about
motherhood and children growing up
-special hand-made cards from the boys
-packing lists
-old jewelry
-my hospital bracelet when John was born
-small change
-paper clips
-baptism candle
-magazine articles on exercise
-washing instruction labels torn out of unknown
garments
-a diary
-movie theater stubs
-Christmas gift lists for every year since 1981
(wow! who the heck is Pam?)
-old photos
-sample tubes of skin cream never opened

I admit there was a little "junk" mixed in. Much of
what I'd held on to for all these years was relinquished
to the waste basket at my side...

ॐ∼ॐ

Rabbit Trails
(A morning in December)

9:00 am and I still haven't had breakfast. But I will now. Wait, I'll call my patient first to confirm her ride tomorrow. The patient tells me she doesn't need the ride after all. Her good friend is coming in from out of town and will take her to her treatment. Okay, I'll wipe it off my dry-erase board on the fridge. Jeez, that board is getting dirty. I'll clean it with nail polish remover. That works well. I'll clean Roby's board, too, while I'm at it. Wait, better write down what's written on them first. I clean the boards. May as well clean the magnetic box that holds the markers. Have to re-write our appointments. I'm getting hungry. Let me put these dirty glasses in the dishwasher, first. Darn, I never emptied the dishwasher last night. May as well empty it now. I pull out the dishes that belong in the corner china closet near the fireplace. Man, that poinsettia on the fireplace has seen better days. There are dropped leaves everywhere! Gotta throw it out. I bring the plant outside to the garbage. I sweep up the dried up leaves on the hearth. I finish emptying the dishwasher. Okay, what do I want for breakfast? Cereal? Eggs? Yogurt? The phone rings. It's Roby. He wants me to get some numbers together for our painter for his taxes. What are you up to, he asks. I'm supposed to be eating breakfast, but I keep getting distracted. Ah, off on rabbit trails, he says. When I hang up, the dryer buzzes. Better get the hanging stuff out right away. I hang some

tops. May as well fold the whole load while I'm here.
It's almost 10:00. Why am I so hungry? Oh, yeah . . . I
haven't had breakfast yet! Roby calls them rabbit trails.
I prefer to call them productive diversions!

ஒ~ல

2015

"*At some point in life
the world's beauty becomes enough.
You don't need to photograph,
paint or even remember it.
It is enough.*"

Toni Morrison

Enough

In the past year or so, I have found myself thinking more and more that it would be quite liberating to just leave my camera home when we go places. I realize that photography is also an art form; I have boxes filled with beautiful matted photos of birds, nature and architecture that I enjoy looking at from time to time. But lately feeding the desire to get that perfect picture feels less gratifying. Is it time to release the need to preserve the moment and instead simply savor it? When I came across this quote recently, I realized that perhaps I'm reaching that point . . . *when the beauty itself is enough.*

⊱⊰

Sitting in Silence

I sit to meditate. Usually I begin with my spiritual readings, then simply sit and send prayers of healing to those people I know who are struggling in some way, either physically or emotionally. Today I thought I would simply sit in silence. I will rest in the moment and calm my mind. I sit quietly. I attach myself to the notion that if I can sit here and release all thought, I will find a sense of peace. I'm certain that I need this peace to feel inner joy.

I count my breaths.
        One . . . . . two . . . . . three . . . . .
Thoughts of the latest social unrest intrude.
I count my breaths.
        One . . . . . two . . . . . three . . . . . four . . . . .
There is so much hatred and misunderstanding in the world.
    Breathe, let go, I tell myself.
        One . . . . two . . . . three . . . . four . . .
Distressing thoughts interfere.
    Concentrate,
        on the in breath, the out breath two . . . three . .
Unrest, anger, intolerance.
There will be no "silence" in my meditation today.
    No peace.
    No joy.

I hear a catbird singing outside the open window.

Such sweet music.

I slowly open my eyes and see the sunshine streaming in across the room.

I feel a sense of peace.

A sense of joy.

And I realize it is always there . . . even in the midst of the turmoil in this world. If we just allow it.

 споро

Joy on the Inside

Often our source of happiness is external. It is dependent on outside circumstances. Our husband brings us flowers. Our team wins the game. We get the job promotion. A bowl of our favorite ice cream! All these things make us happy . . . for a while. Our team loses. We dent the car. A co-worker gossips about us behind our back. These things make us unhappy.

True happiness or joy comes from within. It is rooted in a spiritual sense of well-being. We don't need the approval of others. We don't need a big house or expensive car. We are at peace with who we are, regardless of what happens in our lives. Joy is something we can all cultivate. It comes from a healthy view of ourselves. It comes from a sense of purpose. At any given moment, we can choose joy. Pleasure is fleeting; it comes and goes. But joy, because it is internal, is always there.

৯৯

Lena and Letting Go

Letting go can mean a lot of things. Letting go of bad habits. Letting go of negative attitudes. Letting go of material things. Sometimes letting go means letting go of a way of life, of all that is familiar. And it's a decision we make not because we want to, but because we have no choice.

Seeing the "For Sale" sign in front of Lena's house, I knew it could not have been easy for her to let go. Lena was well into her eighties, if not nineties. With her husband, she'd raised three children in this house. Her oldest were Corine and Patrick. As toddlers, the twins developed physically as expected for their age, but mentally Corine would lag behind. Lena gave birth to another son, Eddy who, like Corine, would be mentally challenged . . . even more so than his older sister.

Lena's house is in our neighborhood. Corine is a tenant in my apartment building, where her parents set her up nearly twenty-five years ago. Lena and her husband wanted their daughter to have some degree of independence. The apartment is just over a mile from their home. Corine works part time cleaning tables and sweeping floors at a local McDonald's. After work she would take the bus to her parents' house, eat dinner and spend time with her family, then take a taxi back to the apartment. Over the years many tenants have come and gone. And the only one that Corine ever felt close to was old Mrs. Clougherty. Corine would buy trinkets at yard sales and give them to Mrs. Clougherty as gifts.

But Mrs. C. moved on to a nursing home more than fifteen years ago and has since died. Except for a friendly hello, no other tenant has since befriended Corine. "Am I your best tenant?" Corine will ask whenever I see her. "Yes, Corine you are," I reassure her. Eddy never left home. When I'd drive by their house, it wasn't unusual to get a friendly wave from Eddy who would be standing in the front of their house, rocking from one foot to the other. My sister, Deb who had worked for a "helping hands" service, had been hired by Lena to take Eddy out once a week. The outing consisted of lunch at Wendy's and shopping at the Goodwill store, a routine that never changed.

Conversations with Lena revealed an interesting and intelligent woman. After her husband died, Lena often took classes at a local senior education center, making arrangements for Eddy while she did so. I have taken an occasional writing class at the center. Lena was more apt to take courses on such things as Russian history or Foreign Relations.

In the past two years Lena's health had become poor. When I had occasion to call her, she'd say that her home was like Grand Central. . . the physical therapist coming to do rehab, the visiting nurse, the housekeeping service. She'd be getting over the flu, or a bout of pneumonia. Corine, she said, was now doing the cooking when she came to visit.

I was walking by Lena's house, shortly after the "For Sale" sign had gone up. Her son Patrick was putting a box in his car. "Your mom is leaving? Where will she be going?" I asked. "To a nice assisted living place in Concord." "Why Concord?" Then Patrick told me that Eddy was no longer living with Lena. She'd made the decision to place him in a residential home for mentally challenged adults. It was on a farm outside of Concord. She wanted to be close to him so that Patrick could bring Eddy to visit her, or vice versa. Knowing how much Eddy hated change or any break from routine, I asked Patrick how he was doing. "He loves it there!"

It must be reassuring to Lena, that Eddy is happy, I thought. But I couldn't imagine how heart breaking it must have been for Lena to make that decision. Eddy has been with her for over fifty years. A sweet kind-hearted man/child who loved Elvis and dancing. Lena was always quick to praise him. Only a couple years prior, she'd been delighted with his total enjoyment of a dancing class he'd been taking for mentally disabled adults. "He looks so forward to it," she'd said. I wondered how lonely it must be for Lena to wake up each morning in that big house without Eddy.

Yet, she'd done what she knew she had to do. She wouldn't be around forever and she needed to be reassured that Eddy would be happy and in good hands before she died. And now the sale of the house was the final test of letting go. Patrick said she was having a difficult time of it. She'd already paid for a month at the assisted living facility, but refused to leave her home. "She just can't do it," he said. "We've moved the furniture and things that she wanted to take with her to her new apartment. It's all ready for her, but she's not budging. We have a service coming in next week to go through the house and take things away for auctioning. We just don't think it'd be a good idea for her to be here for that!"

Later I found out that she did, in fact, leave before that happened. I've since called Lena a number of times. She's adapting, but understandably missing her home. "It's nice that I have my own furniture here, though." she said.

Letting go of some things brings a sense of freedom and well-being, and a fresh start. But sometimes letting go doesn't happen without a lot of heartache. In the end, the sense of peace comes with accepting what we can't change. That is, letting go of the longing and desire for something we can no longer have, and learning to find joy in where we are now.

℺℻

Brussels Sprouts?

"She said to pick whatever we want," I told Roby as we perused my friend Lorraine's vegetable garden. Lorraine and her husband were away in Colorado for a week. "I really want you to pick stuff, it'll go to waste otherwise." she'd told me.

"I wish I knew what all this stuff is!" I said looking at the various greens on the left end of the garden. "I think these might be two different kinds of kale," I mused as I picked some curvy dark greens and some rather flat lighter greens. I stuffed them in the bag I'd brought with me. I broke off a piece of a tall fluffy herb and identified the dill by its smell. I took some dill and some large basil leaves.

"I wonder what this is." I bent down and tugged at some leaves and pulled out a beautiful radish. I picked a couple more. I moved down the row a bit and pulled another. "Whoa, this one is purple. Maybe it's a turnip that has barely grown yet!" I threw it in the bag.

When I got home, I googled images of greens. None of the pictures of kale looked like the flat greens I'd picked. Images of radishes did prove that there are in fact, purple radishes. Since Lorraine had brought a laptop with her, I e-mailed her to ask what the greens at the left of her garden were. "Chard and Kale," she answered. I chopped up the two different greens and cooked them up for dinner.

Two weeks later, Lorraine and her husband were giving us a "tour" of their garden. They explained what the various plants were . . . potatoes, beans, peppers, carrots, eggplant, Brussels sprouts . . .

"Brussels sprouts?" Sure, Lorraine said, noting that the sprouts were just barely beginning to show themselves. I wondered if it was okay to *eat* Brussels sprout leaves.

"I thought you said it was kale?"

"No, the ones at the far left are kale."

"Oh. . . , I thought they were kale. I picked a bunch of the leaves and cooked them up. Sorry!"

Lorraine laughed, "How were they?"

"Not bad."

In the future, I decided, I would not eat anything I couldn't identify.

இஒஇ

Getting in Our Own Way

Have you ever watched a squirrel maneuver from branch to branch, run along the pointy tops of a picket fence, scale a pole or walk a wire with the agility of a tightrope walker. Have you ever wondered how birds can fly so swiftly through the trees without hitting a branch. Animals don't stop to think "I can't do this" or "I might fall or get hurt".

Man is supposedly more intelligent. But I wonder sometimes if our ability to "think" doesn't get in the way of doing all that we are truly capable of. Our fears and insecurities stem from our thoughts, not our lack of potential. We analyze too much. We compare too much. We judge too much. We worry too much. Simply, we think too much! How much more we are able to accomplish when we proceed with an innate confidence, leaving doubt out of the equation.

ॐॐ

Beginning of August 2015

Maybe I'm being childish and a bit selfish but I can't help being disappointed. It began with our back neighbors cutting down their tree. A large tree . . . on the back property line. A tree, that years ago I'd begrudged for slowly taking away the sun that nourished my back gardens. But over the years, I'd grown to love the green coolness. We'd even begun to embrace the moss that is beginning to take over what was once a lawn. The moss is green, after all, and doesn't need mowing.

Suddenly our cool sheltered back yard is again awash with sunshine. Only now it feels like an intrusion. Where I'd grown to feel a sense of being in a soothing oasis, I now feel exposed. And I'm beginning to wonder what made us decide to put a fence back there. I guess we wanted to rid ourselves of the bushes around the edge of the yard that had grown ugly and sparse in the years of shade. Did we think we could bring back the feeling of coziness the tree and the bushes had provided? Now it looks sterile. I torture myself by pulling out photos of the yard *with* the tree, *with* the bushes, *without* the fence!

Two weeks later . . .

I know that nothing stays the same forever and that change is inevitable . . . a fact that I need to accept. So, I've tried to see the advantages of having a sunny backyard. Roby and I have cleared off a large area where I will plant wildflower seeds. I once had a wildflower garden back there; why not again? And Roby's always wished to have a spot to grow a few tomatoes and cucumbers. So he set up a small raised garden, ready for planting in the spring.

Late fall . . .

With gratitude for the absence of the big tree that once produced so many leaves that needed raking and with appreciation for the fence that keeps neighbors leaves out of our yard, Roby is enjoying how much less work the fall clean up has been.

I won't say I don't still miss the feel of the once shady yard, but I know with the growth of new plantings, the backyard will slowly regain it's sense of peace and comfort.

ॐ∽

Good Tea

There is nothing like cleaning out closets and cupboards to reacquaint ourselves with things that had somehow been pushed far to the back, out of sight and mind. Such was the case with the tin of expensive loose green tea that David and Leliah had given me last Christmas. It takes slightly longer to prepare, but the enjoyment well worth it. It makes you wonder how many other things lie hidden and forgotten. Not just things, but are there people in our lives who we've pushed back in our minds and haven't taken the time to remember and enjoy? All it takes is a phone call to say . . . "I've been thinking about you. How are you?"

ॐॐ

A Winter Walk in Late Afternoon

At this time of year, the sun sits low in the sky
And I follow my shadow, far taller than I
The hill is steep and my stride is slow
But my shadow is patient even though.
It slows its pace in step with mine
Not in a hurry, I take my time
It knows that, for me, this solitary stroll
Is less for my body than it is for my soul.

I let go of thoughts of chores undone
Of errands that I will have to run.
Releasing my worries, I choose to be free.
In this moment I am simply happy to be.

We round a bend and now I see
My shadow walking alongside of me
I study its silhouette and note with a grin
The fray on my boot where fake fur once had been
Another turn in the road
And we head downhill
Out of sight is my shadow
But with me still
On cloudy days I walk alone
But today my shadow follows me home.

෨෧

2016

*At our center is our authentic self. The self unblemished
and unaffected by that which is outside of ourselves.
It is where compassion and connection to others lie.
It is where we are whole.
There is abundant joy to be found at our center.*

Thank You for Staying

As I sit quietly reading, I hear the Carolina Wren in the tree outside the window. "Thank you for staying" I say to him. Until the past few years, I'd never heard this bird song in my backyard. I'd heard it many times up at the campground in Moultonboro. And for years, I had looked to the trees to see what bird produced this sweet melodic sound. I never did find him.

And then one day I heard it. That lovely song here in my own backyard. And finally discovered who sang it. I'd thought the Carolina Wrens might just be passing through. But they've stayed. Nesting here, visiting my feeder and delighting me with their song.

ᐛ

Spark of Divinity in Our Hearts

Mahatma Gandhi said, "*I do dimly perceive that whilst everything around me is ever changing, ever dying, there is underlying all that change, a living power that is changeless, that holds all together, that creates, dissolves, and re-creates. That informing power or spirit is God. . . . Hence I gather that God is Life, Truth, Light. He is Love. He is the supreme Good.*"

For me, this is a simple, but powerful description of the supreme reality that most of the world's great religions call God. The spiritual teacher, Eknath Easwaran spoke of "*an incomparable spark of divinity is to be found in the heart of each human being, waiting to radiate love and wisdom everywhere, because that is its nature.*" When we seek God, we seek what already lies within us. Life, truth, light, love. The more we nurture our true selves, the more attentive we are to our spiritual nature, the more we will find the peace and wisdom that our inner being already possesses.

❧

Do You have any Grandchildren?

This is the question that women my age get whenever we run into an acquaintance we haven't seen in a while. I detect a look of pity when I say no. I tell them that, of course I'd be thrilled to become a grandmother, who wouldn't? But my happiness doesn't depend on it. I have a full life; I'm content, I'm happy. If it never happens, that's okay. They are never convinced and try to assure me: "Don't worry. It's never too late. They may surprise you."

I enjoy listening to my friends' stories about their own grandkids and can see the pleasure it brings. But why would I live with a sense of "something missing" when I have so much to be grateful for? I have been blessed with three sons. I enjoy a great relationship with each one. That is an incredible gift. And that is enough.

૱ન્

Meh

My friend, Carol told me of a new saying her husband has. In the past his favorite saying was, "It is what it is." His new one is . . . simply . . . "meh". When you can't change something, I guess "It is what it is." When it's insignificant . . . "Meh." Like when someone does or says something that you may not agree with, but it's not important enough to make a fuss about, so you just let it go.

Today when I drove my cancer patient, he was quite verbal about all the ills of the world and had solutions for all of them. His "solutions" were fraught with unrealistic expectations and lack of knowledge of the circumstances. I was inclined to point out the folly of his thinking. Instead I just listened and to myself said, "Meh."

સ્જ

Healing

There have been a number of acts of terrorism in recent months all over the world. I think of the evil in this world and I wonder how we can possibly stop it. In World War II, we fought on the battlefields and we knew who our enemy was. Today it's not so clear. I grapple with what the future of humankind looks like.

I recall 9-11 and how we watched the news for weeks and months as the cleanup took place, as people tried to put their lives back together. It seemed as though we would never recover. Then I think of our trip to New York City in 2011, ten years later. David's apartment at the time was in Jersey City, directly across the Hudson River from where the Twin Towers had stood. A new skyscraper, nearly three quarters to completion, now rose in their place. And I'm reminded that throughout the existence of mankind, war and persecution, floods, earthquakes and other tragic events have plagued the world. And always, man has persevered and in time, recovered.

We can't take away the pain and anguish of those affected by tragedy. But we can see how the community of man, in the midst of a disaster, comes together unified and strong to help one another. I am encouraged by the innate goodness of the human spirit that shines through in the wake of tragedy, and by man's ability to heal.

෨෧

How do You Reconcile
Your Beliefs with Roby's?

This is the question my best friend Carol asked me recently. Roby is Christian; I lean toward Buddhist philosophy. So Carol was curious.

I told her we respect and honor each other's freedom to follow our own spiritual path without judgment or feeling that our own path is the only right one. Sometimes Roby and I will take the time to each read from our own spiritual books, then talk about what resonated with us from our reading, how a passage may have caused us to stop and reflect on its meaning in our own life. Often the passages we've chosen to share are strikingly similar. The spiritual journey for each of us is a very personal one, yet we've discovered that regardless of the religious tradition, the wisdom and lessons of love and compassion are the same.

ॐ

A Lesson in Humility

I finish the first song. No applause. Wait . . . one or two people are clapping. Then they stop, realizing they are the only ones. No applause?? This has never happened before. "Don't they like me?" "Am I that bad?" It's an uncomfortable feeling when no one applauds. It does something to your psyche. I look at Roby. He raises his eyebrows. Though I remind everyone that they are welcome to sing along, my second song brings a lukewarm response. The activities director looks embarrassed. During the third song, she tries to spark some life and enthusiasm in her people.

Mostly we perform for independent senior living places. Today we are at a nursing home and I recognize that they may not be in the best health. I remind myself why I'm there. Not for the applause, but to bring the gift of these old songs to the residents. I let go of my insecurities and warm up to the audience. I look out at their faces and I see some smiles. Some are quietly singing along. Others are tapping their feet.

Midway through the program, Roby tells his jokes. Silence. "Tough crowd", we silently communicate to each other in bemusement. Later, the activities director would tell us that many of the attendees had been sitting out in the warm sun, only to be brought into the air-conditioning for the show and had complained of being cold.

Although they were not a demonstrative audience, at the end many tell us how much they enjoyed the music and that they hope we'll come back.

Still, having a taste of "humble pie" was not a bad thing.

৯৯৯

New York City

"Ah, this is the way to travel!" I said to Roby. We were on an Amtrak train traveling to New York City from Boston. Michael was with us, too. We had planned a long family weekend with his brothers. We hadn't been to New York in four years and they'd asked us numerous times when we were going to visit them again. John and Colette lived in Brooklyn; David and Leliah in Manhattan's Upper East Side. As badly as I wanted to go, I had resisted making plans because I dreaded the drive to and into the big City. With each passing year I've become more of a basket case on major highways. I don't like the busyness and speed of all the cars around me, even if I'm not the one driving. When Roby suggested taking a train, I was all for it.

At one time I had no interest in visiting New York City. The thought of it frightened me. I visualized a big scary place where you could never feel safe. That changed in 2006. Several months after my husband Lou died, I had an opportunity to go with two friends. Joan had invited Lorraine and me to accompany her to New York to hear her daughter sing in a Jazz club on Friday night. At first I declined. But remembering I now lived alone and there was nothing keeping me from going, I had no excuse. Joan loved New York City and was fearless navigating the streets.

When we left the nightclub, we made our way to a popular café. And as we walked the streets, I saw that New York was not the scary place I'd envisioned.

Over coffee and pastry, we made a unanimous decision to stay an extra night, to avail ourselves of some sightseeing the next day. It was late when we finally left the café. As we headed to Brooklyn where we were to spend the night at our kids' apartments, my cell phone rang. It was John. "Mom, where are you? It's late, I was worried about you!" I had to laugh. Our roles had been reversed.

The next day John and I went out for breakfast. Like many in the City, he didn't own a car. As we walked down the street, he pointed out his grocery store, his laundromat, his favorite deli, his favorite breakfast place, and where he got the subway into Manhattan to go to work. I came to realize that if you lived in Brooklyn and Manhattan, it was not so impersonal after all. The blocks that surround your apartment become your neighborhood. And at the places you frequent, the vendors get to know you. Something that is missing in our suburbs, as we get in our cars and drive to multiple places to do our shopping.

I've come to enjoy the City in the years since, and now on the train I could enjoy a stress free commute. From Penn Station it might have been doable to walk to our hotel. But our luggage was cumbersome (I always overpack) and a line of taxis were there waiting for us. I'd been on the subways, but had never been in a New York City cab. Everything I'd heard about their driving was true. And despite my occasional gasps and internal dialogue, *"my Gawd, what is he doing? Doesn't he realize this is a one lane road, not two? .... how does he plan to merge in? ...aaaah...OMG!....okay.....he's good, I'm okay"*, I put my trust in our driver explicitly.

For the next four days, we enjoyed the City. Saturday was spent in Brooklyn, where John and Colette planned a full day. Prospect Park in the afternoon, dinner at their apartment and an evening of entertainment at a venue unlike any I'd been to. When you enter the old brick building that houses the Jalopy Theater, you feel like you've stepped back in time, the rustic stage, the church bench seats and more magically --- the music. Jalopy features traditional roots music, folk, country and bluegrass. That night a husband and wife duo entertained us with some traditional bluegrass songs, he on guitar and banjo, she on fiddle. They sang old ballads passed down through generations, and I felt as though I were in Appalachia, not Brooklyn. A large venue with a famous singer would not have brought me as much pleasure as our evening at Jalopy.

Sunday included Central Park, which was not too far from where David and Leliah were currently living. It was a beautiful fall day and we did trails in the Park we hadn't been to before. Later in the afternoon Roby and I parted ways with the kids; they headed to the Central Park Zoo; we headed back to Midtown. We had tickets for a musical that evening, our first Broadway show. Several months earlier, I bought tickets to "Carole King, the Musical". Some of the bigger shows were either booked or terribly expensive. We were not disappointed. We enjoyed the acting, the music and just the fact that we were finally at a Broadway show.

Monday we visited the National September 11 Memorial, a tribute to the nearly 3,000 people who died when the World Trade Center's Twin Towers were attacked by terrorists in 2001. The twin reflecting pools, formed by the 30 ft. waterfalls cascading down the sides, sit where the Towers once stood. The bronze panels edging the Memorial pools, bear the names of every person who died. It was sobering to see.

The afternoon was spent in Midtown sightseeing. We visited the New York Public Library, St. Patrick's Cathedral and Rockefeller Center. That day, the kids were "tourists" right along with us, seeing places they'd been meaning to visit since they moved to New York years earlier. We capped the evening off at a fine Italian restaurant and then a stroll down Times Square. There is no place quite like Times Square at night. The bright lights, marquees and colorful billboards and of course, the people. It's exhilarating just to be there among tourists from all over the world.

After hugs and goodbyes at the Subway station, I walked back to the hotel with Roby and Michael, feeling melancholy, as I always do at the end of a visit with my kids.

æ∞

Leora

As co-director of the Hospice Choir, I am always invited to attend the last class of the latest graduates of the Hospice Volunteer training sessions. Those of us that head up one of the many different programs that new volunteers can consider as they decide in what capacity they wish to volunteer, speak about what our program is all about. At a recent graduation, as I was reminded of all the volunteer possibilities there were, I wondered if it was time I did more than just sing with the choir. I feel a calling to working more directly with some of the patients either with one on one visitations, or Life's Journey which involves speaking with the patients about their life and then compiling these remembrances in the form of a written booklet to be passed on to the families after the patient dies. I wonder if I'm ready. And then Leora comes to mind.

Lea was a tenant of mine for years. Almost as far back as when Lou first bought the building. Twenty years? Twenty-five? She remained until she ended up in a nursing home. Lea was a widow when she moved into our apartment. She and her husband had never been blessed with children. I always thought her to be a classy lady. Not in the way she dressed or her appearance; she was a simple woman. But in her demeanor. She was smart, modest, always pleasant, interesting to talk to. She would sometimes invite me into her apartment for tea. She'd apologize for her apartment being messy, referring to the piles of paperwork and mail by her recliner. "That's where I sit to pay my bills," she would explain.   When my boys were teenagers and worked at the building doing raking or vacuuming the hallways, Lea would offer them lemonade. She was never one to complain or speak ill of anyone. Until she entered the nursing home . . .

Initially, Lea was in the nursing home for rehab, recovering from a car accident she'd been in. "I didn't want George to drive my car, but he insisted," Lea told me. "He'd already had near accidents, but he would *not* let me drive." George was a gentleman friend of Lea's. I'd never heard this bitterness in her voice.

I continued to visit Lea often. She had a beloved sister and grown nieces who were dear to her and she to them, but they all lived in Massachusetts. They came when they could, but with jobs and children of their own, it was not frequent. Lea's sister, Mary still lived in her own home, but was getting on in years herself and not very mobile. But she and Lea spoke on the phone once or twice a week.

My visits with Lea were delightful. She would regale me with stories of her younger days. She'd grown up in Littleton, a small rural town in northern New Hampshire. She spoke of barn dances, visits to Canada to visit relatives, hard times when "new clothes" were dresses made by her mother from old drapes. She spoke fondly of her family, sisters and brothers. All were gone now except for Mary.

Lea was as sharp as ever. She would relate in detail what each of her nieces, husbands and children were currently engaged in.   "Annie's son Luke is in his first year at B.U. . . ." "Laura's husband is traveling to Thailand with his job . . . " She'd ask me about my boys, what they were up to, what was new with Roby and me.

Weeks would go by until I visited again and she'd remember everything I'd told her, taking great pleasure in hearing about our lives.

But some conversations revealed things I'd never known about her relationship with George. How happy I had been when she'd found a male companion. How nice, I'd thought, of George to pick her up at the apartment building to take her to church or to go shopping. The truth, as Lea now confided, was that George was controlling. He made decisions for her. He'd demeaned her. Told her to change if he didn't approve of what she was wearing. He'd honk impatiently in the parking lot if she wasn't outside waiting for him. The more I learned about George, the more I hurt inside for Lea. I'd had no idea. She'd never said anything. I imagine her pride prevented her from admitting that this man was controlling her. I suspected that those closest to her had warned her. But now she was angry. She wanted never to see him again. And she never did.

Lea was not recovering fully and she didn't want to be a burden on her family in Massachusetts. She thought it best for all concerned to give up the apartment and just remain in the nursing home. I was never sure she made the right decision.

Lea seldom left her room. She seemed resigned to her circumstances, while managing to maintain a grateful attitude. If an aid came in to check on her while I was there, Lea would introduce me enthusiastically as her dear, dear friend. And she'd likewise sing the praises of the aide, thanking them for taking such good care of her. I would offer to find a way to take Lea out, take a walk in the park across the street, feel the fresh air. How she enjoyed gazing out at the park, watching the birds or a wedding party being photographed near the flowering bushes. But she refused. Just the thought of it tired her.

As the years passed, Lea's eyesight and trembling hands prevented her from writing letters. Talking on the phone was becoming difficult, so her chats with Mary were slowly ending. She'd often say to me, "Well, there is one thing I can still do. And that is pray! I think that's why God is keeping me here. I pray for all the people I know." She told me every time I visited that she kept me and my family in her daily prayers.

Why does Leora come to mind as I muse the possibility of taking on a more intimate role as a Hospice volunteer? Because I feel that I failed Lea in her final months. As she deteriorated, I visited less often. She'd become confused. Her bright blue eyes had dimmed. Her smile all but gone. She spoke painfully slow and her speech was difficult to understand. I didn't know what to do. What to say. How would I respond if I didn't know what she was saying? What if engaging her in conversation was too tiring for her? I tried singing to her, but couldn't tell if she enjoyed it or if it agitated her.

Lea had often said that she was ready for God to take her. Now I prayed He would. And I felt guilty... did I want her to die because I knew she would be in a better place, and with those she loved? Or because I wouldn't have to feel guilty every time I passed Mt. Carmel Nursing home and didn't stop to visit her. At her funeral, her family sought me out. They said they'd heard so much about me and thanked me profusely for being such a good friend to Aunt Leora. I muttered something about not visiting as often as I should have, but they'd hear none of it. "You were here when we couldn't be. We are so grateful for that. Thank you!" Their gratitude did little to alleviate the feeling that I hadn't done enough.

Now I have a chance to try again. Unlike many people I know, relating to frail older people has never been a comfortable thing for me. But Hospice training has taught me that being there for someone isn't about me or whether or not I'm saying or doing the "right" thing. It's about giving someone your whole-hearted attention. It's holding a hand. Looking into a person's eyes and seeing not their frailness or their aged face, but their soul. It's letting go of expectations and just letting your heart lead the way.

I still have so much to learn about how to love; maybe my Hospice patients can teach me.

෴

Does it Spark Joy?

That is the question that Marie Kondo, who wrote "The Life-Changing Magic of Tidying Up" suggests you ask yourself when you are trying to decide whether something should be kept or not. Let's face it. We all tend to keep far more than we have any use for. We set out to purge our belongings with the best intentions only to have our efforts thwarted by the "past" and "future" dilemma. Much of what we hold on to is either tied to the past - it holds sentimental value; or it is tied to the future - we may need it someday! Marie tells us to hold the object in your hand and ask yourself "does it spark joy"?

I admit, I thought that sounded a bit corny. But I decided to try it. Of course, the book uses other criteria to consider when making decisions. And there are different chapters for clothes, books, paperwork, toiletries, kitchen, etc. But the "joy" factor plays into all of them. I decided to start with my books.

We have a finished basement. One room had five bookcases filled with books. I doubted I could part with any of them. Two of those bookcases contained children's books, along with collections of humor books ("Far Side" "Foxtrot", etc.) that the boys had enjoyed in their teen years. I hadn't been able to part with them all these years; why should it be any different now?

I removed each book one by one and held it. Did it spark joy? Sometimes the answer was "Yes!" It may have been a favorite book I used to read to the boys when they were little, a book they still spoke fondly of as adults. So it went in the "Keep" pile. Others, though great kids' books, held no special sentimental value. I'd held on to them in anticipation of someday reading them to my grandchildren. I came to the realization that I may never have grandchildren and if I do, I'll buy new books. And that there are families and children out there who could be enjoying these books now! These went in the "Donate" pile. When I held the humor books, I found that while "Calvin and Hobbs" sparked joy, "Far Side" didn't and so on. Marie Kondo's method worked. When I was done, I had gone from seven shelves of kids' books to two and a half! I disposed of one bookcase and used the empty shelves of the other for board games (disposing of the three shelf cupboard that had housed the games). I donated the younger kids' books to a non-profit that worked with un-wed moms. They were thrilled. I continued with my own books and ended up with more empty shelves that I now use for photo albums.

I've used the "joy" method with my clothes, too. Even when shopping for new clothes, I ask myself if it sparks joy or am I just "settling" on it because I can't seem to find what I really want. I've learned from experience that "settling" results in clothes that I seldom, if ever wear.

I've taken the concept a step further. It can also apply to how we use our time. I have spent a ridiculous amount of time surfing the web. Does this sound familiar? You go on-line to look something up. For me it may be to hear a song on youtube. Which leads to checking out more songs that are on the sidebar. That leads to watching an interview of one of the singers singing the song from the sidebar, which (and I can't explain how this happens) eventually leads to watching cute videos of babies and animals! Then you realize that you just wasted an hour (or more). I say "waste" because I know there were more fulfilling ways I could have spent that time. Which isn't to say you can't enjoy a funny video or two. But we often get drawn in and become addicted. In the end, I don't feel a sense of satisfaction. I'm getting better at stopping to think about what I'm doing. And yes, asking myself, "Does it spark joy?"

இ௸

Mom's Bookcase

Aside from those that held the children's books, I have a special bookcase that is oak with glass doors. When I was a child, the shelves held a set of encyclopedias and hardcover sets of the classics - "A Tale of Two Cities", "Tom Sawyer", "Jane Eyre" and "Wuthering Heights" to name a few. I read many of them along with my Nancy Drews and Happy Hollisters. Mom acquired the encyclopedias one book a week at the local supermarket. That was a big thing back in the 50's. If you spent so much on groceries, you acquired the feature of the week at a good price. That is how we came to own the Classics as well. I loved to read and lose myself in a good story. It is only now, looking back, that I can truly appreciate having these books available to me as a child.

Over the years, I came to have only six of the books in these collections in my possession. I also rescued several of the Nancy Drews from a yard sale Mom had a few years after I left home. My youngest brother (still a kid at the time) was hoping to reap some profit from them. How dare he --- they were *my* books.

In her later years, Mom used the bookcase to showcase her doll collection. When she died, the bookcase was left to my sister, Jayne. I was disappointed. Whether my sisters and brothers had the same affinity for books that I did, I don't remember, but I'd always thought of the bookcase as mine. Because Jayne had daughters, I imagine Mom intended the bookcase to be used to house the dolls that had been left to my nieces. My disappointment was brief. I was happy to know the bookcase would still be in the family.

It wasn't until years later, in the midst of a separation and impending move, my sister decided that the bookcase, amongst other things, would have to go. "I want you to have it," Jayne said to me, "I know you always loved it." Had my feelings been that evident when Mom died? Now I felt bad. "When things settle down," I told her, "you can have it back". "That's okay," she said, "someday I'd like something a bit nicer for the dolls."

I filled the bookcase, lovingly putting the old books back on the shelves where they once sat, adding those I'd acquired over the years. I couldn't help feeling that the bookcase was where it belonged. Occasionally I still pull out "The Family Book of Best Loved Poems". I sit and read and discover again poems I remember enjoying as a child.

చ్

Last January I had tried my hand at water colors. I watched youtube tutorials on watercolor painting. I studied techniques for wispy, airy renditions of flowers and animals. I bought the suggested paper, brushes and colors. I set up a space to work at in the basement. I arranged all the supplies. I wanted to get started. But every time I sat myself down in front of my paper, I froze. A week went by before I actually took brush to paper.

I made the mistake they'd warned about in the videos; I used too much water. The colors were too diluted. The paper too wet. I decided to have some of my cheaper art paper on the side to test the colors and wetness before painting on my good sheet. I tried to produce a simple picture in the delicate airy style I so admired. The little vase didn't look half bad, but the teacup next to it only became more and more muddy looking as I tried in vain to "correct" my mistakes. Frustrated, I took some red and in a circular motion made it an apple. An ugly mucky looking apple. Days later when I showed my attempt to my son Michael, he said he liked it. I pointed to the apple and said "that was supposed to be a teacup!" "I still like it," he said. "You can have it if you want," I told him. "Really, are you sure?" he asked. Beauty is in the eye of the beholder, as they say.

I didn't give up. I looked through some of my photos for subjects to paint. I chose some birds. I was still aiming for the wispy freestyle effect, where just a few strokes and a few splashes of color would create the desired image. But I couldn't resist zeroing in on the details. Fine lines for the feathers, the beak and the eye, the clear definition of the tree branches. I did several birds in the same fashion. Considering I hadn't painted since some art classes in my teens, and this had been my first serious attempt using watercolors, the results weren't half bad.

I'm still determined to learn how to paint with more freedom, using fewer strokes and letting go of the need for detail. I know it will take a bit of practice to achieve the effortless, airy effect I want. I'm reminded of my attempts to create a wildflower garden, or a least a somewhat "wild" garden. Not that my gardens aren't lovely. But I've always been drawn to the natural feel of wild gardens. But my need for some kind of order and symmetry always sabotages my efforts.

Is it possible to change my painting style? If my attempt at wild gardening is any indication, maybe not. That won't deter me from trying again, though.

அ~ஓ

Writing: An Exercise in Mindfulness

Once it seemed important to have that close up "frame worthy" shot of the heron gliding over the water. Or a picture of the flock of cedar waxwings in the berry bush. Or multiple photos to document the wedding of a friend's child.

I have been slowly letting go of the need to photograph every nature shot and every social event I attend. A single group shot of a birthday or get-together is enough to recall the date it took place and who was there. Except for the photos of the kids growing up, which we revisit and enjoy, many of the other photos I've taken over the years are far less important now.

Writing has become more satisfying for me than photography. I can look at a photo that I've taken and the photo will tell me what I've seen. But to *write* of what I've seen brings back more than a picture in my mind; it invites me to relive the moment, taking the time to find just the right words; words that evoke not only an image, but all the senses and the emotions that went with it.

That is what I feel when I read my son Michael's poetry. Poetry is what grows from the seeds of mindfulness and connection to life as it happens. A simple observation from his balcony becomes a poem, and when I read it, a picture is created in my mind and I am there . . . living that moment so eloquently captured, not with a camera but with just a few words.

ॐॐ

Passion

We all need something to be passionate about. I believe it's a fundamental need of all human beings. Whether its devoting time to a hobby, learning or discovering something new or volunteering . . . finding something to be passionate about can bring you out of yourself, into a place that is fulfilling and nourishing to your soul. Roby urges the men in his monthly men's grief group to find something satisfying to do. While they will never stop missing their wives or partners, it doesn't mean that life has to stop.

"I want to try surfing again!" Ron announced at the September meeting. In his mid-seventies and widowed a year earlier, Ron had lived in California in his younger days and enjoyed surfing. The reaction was understandable. "Are you kidding?" "At your age?" "So you're going to California?" No, Ron wasn't going to California. People do surf on the coast of New Hampshire.

A few weeks later, Ron called Roby to give him a website link to see photos of him surfing. He'd hooked up with a young man who taught surfing on the coast, who was more than happy to help Ron get back to surfing, renting him the gear, and giving him a refresher course. The pictures were amazing. They showed Ron sitting on his board paddling out to the waves, getting up, then riding the waves. The last was a picture of Ron and the young instructor standing side by side, still in wetsuits holding up their surfboards.

At the next men's group meeting, Roby brought his laptop and pulled up the pictures to show the group. Ron enjoyed the attention and the admiration of the other men. But the most wonderful thing was the effect that following his passion had had on him. The evidence was in the broad smile on his face and the sparkle in his eyes which hadn't been there until now.

৵৽৹

What if . . .

At church, the pastor posed this question: What if tomorrow you were left with *only* the things you are grateful for today?   On the way home, I thought about that question. *Are we* always grateful for the blessings we have in our life? Imagine that today you are angry at your spouse and not the least bit appreciative of the things you *do* love about him.   Or perhaps today you really take your health for granted. After all you eat right and exercise, you tell yourself.   Not like Joe next door who deserves all his health problems, considering how overweight he is and he eats the wrong food, after all. Tomorrow comes and the husband you were angry with is gone; you are a widow. Your physical well-being has been compromised because of a bad fall; you are in great pain and can hardly walk.

Of course, these things won't happen just because of your attitude.   Still, there *is* something lost when we don't live each moment with a thankful heart.   Our relationships suffer.   Our spiritual well-being suffers.

"What if?"   It's a question worth reflecting on.

ॐ≈

A Gift

"Would you like to come in when I ring the bell?"

I have met some pretty amazing people as a cancer driver. Sandra was one of them. I'd driven her to several of her radiation treatments. She was always upbeat and cheerful; even the one time she said she was kind of depressed, she managed to joke around. She referred to herself as the old bald lady in her complex. She was always so appreciative of the rides. Though I was certain that I was not her favorite driver. She often spoke of that nice male driver with the Australian accent.

Two weeks earlier, when I was sitting in the waiting room waiting for Sandra, another cancer patient who always came in moments after her, was greeted by the two receptionists with cheers and applause. It was this gentleman's final radiation treatment. "Wow, what a greeting!" he said to his friend who always drove him. (I would miss seeing this patient, or more accurately "hearing" him speak. I loved his voice. He was a rather tall and husky man in his 70's whose voice, rich and deep, commanded respect and attention . . . a radio voice.) Radio voice had gifts for each of the ladies. "There's no calories!" he said as he handed them what I'm guessing were chocolates or baked goods. When they thanked him and said he shouldn't have, he said that they'd been wonderful to him and it was just a token of his appreciation. I knew that the celebratory mood would continue in the back room. I'd heard that patients were invited to ring a bell to ceremoniously commemorate the end of their treatments.

This day, Sandra had brought a friend of hers who lived in the same housing building. It was Sandra's final treatment. I had hoped to be the one to drive her on her last trip up the hill to the Cancer center at the Elliot Hospital. "Man it'll be nice to be able to sleep in again. Getting up early every morning for the last five weeks for these treatments has been brutal." "Yeah, well." her friend said, "I'm gonna call you at 6:00 am and wake you up anyway!" "Do that and I'll throw you out the window!" Sandra fired back. The banter between them was indicative of the comfortable and playful relationship they shared. Sandra had invited her friend because she wanted her there when she rang the bell. Then she asked if I'd like to be there, too. I hadn't expected her to invite me, and I felt honored.

Sandra disappeared down the hall as her friend and I sat in the waiting room, only to quickly reappear with a bag of Lindt chocolates. "Look what they gave me!" She handed them to her friend to hold for her. "And don't touch them! Or I'll kill you!" she said in her crusty voice. Her friend laughed when she left and told me, "She knows I don't eat chocolates."

A short time later we were called back by one of the nurses. We waited in the hall that abutted the radiation room, along with half a dozen staff. When Sandra emerged into the hallway, everyone cheered her. And when she rang the bell, tears ran down her friend's face. "For Pete's sake," Sandra said to her, "You're worse than I am!" Everyone hugged Sandra and she was visibly moved by all the attention.

Back in the car, I gave Sandra a card and small tin of Christmas cookies I'd made. Her hands were full with all the exit paperwork and gifts that had been given to her. I found a bag in my trunk, "Here, you can carry your stuff in it," I told her. Which was a good thing, because as we neared her apartment building, she asked me to drop them off a block before. "We're stopping at the Bar for a drink to celebrate!" Sandra said. The bartender, she said, would be happy for her.

She thanked me again for doing what I do. I wished her luck and a healthy future. "Yeah, well I guess I should stop smoking," she said unconvincingly as she waved goodbye. I smiled as I drove off, happy to have met this likable character and quite certain she would not change her ways.

ॐॐ

Touching Pearl

It was December. Our Hospice singing group was singing Christmas songs for a group of patients at a local nursing facility. Pearl was among the residents that had been brought to the community room to hear us. We were in the dementia unit. Some of us knew Pearl. Like us, she'd been a Hospice volunteer. But Alzheimer's had changed the course of her life and it was sad to see her now. Slumped in her wheelchair, eyes barely open, she was in her own world, seemingly unaware of us.

The other patients were in various stages of dementia. When we began to sing the familiar songs, the more alert ones happily sang along. And slowly with each song, more of them showed recognition, singing along quietly. Even Pearl began to mouth the words, though her eyes remained closed. Those of us who knew her looked at each other and smiled. By the time we ended our last song, Pearl's eyes were open and she was smiling. It was a special moment. It would seem, that while other things may be lost, the ravages of dementia cannot take away that place within a person that is touched by music.

❧❦

---

*"As we get older, character becomes etched on our face.
Beautiful old people are works of art. Like a white candle
in a holy place, so is the beauty of an aged face."*

James Simpson

Visitations

I went for my first Hospice (one on one) patient visitation today. It was a training really, with Marilyn, the hospice volunteer who heads up the nursing home ministry. We currently have two hospice patients at this nursing facility at which I've been assigned.

We visited each patient; both diagnosed with Alzheimer's. Dolly was verbal, though not coherent. But she offered a smile here and there. June said little and looked at us suspiciously; she seemed not at all comfortable with the attention we were giving her.

Marilyn asked the ladies some simple questions, trying to stimulate conversation. To her questions, Dolly could only say, "I don't know." June simply looked baffled, not comprehending the questions. I suppose that Marilyn wasn't really familiar with Dolly and June. The nursing home where Marilyn does her own visitations is not this one. It was evident that these ladies were deep in the throws of Alzheimer's. I'm not sure what my approach will be --- maybe just sit and possibly share photos or music with them --- whatever seems to reach them. I am prepared to acknowledge that I may never be able to reach them.

Seeing what Alzheimer's does to people is heartbreaking. The visit saddened me but did not discourage me. Dolly and June will not remember me next time I visit, but I wonder if maybe they have something to teach me.

ॐ

Last Night's Dream

I dreamt that Roby and I were at someone's home for a get together. I don't know who the people were; even in the dream it didn't seem we knew them all that well. As we were mingling, someone announced that Lou was coming. Lou? Everyone appeared happy about this, like they all knew him. And then, Diana (Lou's sister) and Lou's mom walked in. This, too, was a surprise as Mom had died 4 years ago. And then Lou entered the room. Locking eyes and smiling, we made our way to one another. A hug and a gentle kiss. And then I awoke.

It seemed as though our encounter had been more like long lost friends . . . not lovers. As though we both knew my romantic feelings now belonged to someone else. To Roby. In the dream I was concerned that Roby would feel cast aside. But I sensed that even Lou knew and accepted that that couldn't be further from the truth.

๖๏๑

A Return to Love

At one time I would use a highlighter to mark the quotes or paragraphs that resonated with me in a book. But I've learned that when I go back to read those same lines years or even weeks later, they often don't affect me quite as they did then. What was powerful when I first read it, isn't necessarily what I need now.

I refrain from marking my books now, using little post-its instead, that can easily be removed. Which is a good thing, because there are very few pages unmarked in "A Return to Love" by Marianne Williamson, my current read. I love the lessons and pearls of wisdom in this book.

Today I was reading a chapter on "Work". To quote Marianne: *"Don't ask God to send you a brilliant career, but rather ask Him to show you the brilliance within you. . . . Achievement doesn't come from what we do, but from who we are."* She talks about living our lives in accordance with who we are, not with what others expect us to be. Marianne reminds us that no matter what we do, we can make it our ministry. Whether we are an elevator operator or the CEO of a large corporation, there is no one whose job is more important than another's. No matter what we are doing, we all have the same power and potential to spread love and light to others.

A while back, when my son, Michael and I were talking about this subject, he said how he still remembers fondly one of the kitchen staff at the UNH cafeteria when he was in college. She seemed to love what she was doing. She was always cheerful and had a way of making everyone feel good, lifting you up even if you were having a bad day.

I think we can all go back in our lives and bring to mind those people who had a way of making us feel good about ourselves. Back before I had children and was still working full time, my husband Lou and I would have breakfast once a week at Blake's restaurant before heading to work. One of my co-worker's mom was always there and we would chat briefly before finding our table. She was elderly and by society's definition, a plain, simple woman. I always looked forward to seeing her. She had a way of making you feel special and important. Her warmth and positive nature, indeed the very essence of her being has to this day left a lasting impression on my heart.

No matter who we are or what we do, we can be a spark of light in somebody's day.

ॐॐ

The Visits

It is spring and I've been visiting our Hospice patients for a few months now. We currently have six patients at the facility I've been assigned. Dolly and June are still with us. I've managed to awaken some responses from Dolly; she enjoyed the garden images I pulled up on my tablet. Often I hear Dolly before I see her. She loves to sing. The words make no sense, but her singing makes me smile. June is always sleeping and the only reaction I get from her is an occasional flicker of her eyes opening.

I began to note the different stages of Alzheimer's. June and Dolly have passed the stage of being aware of their confusion, which I have to think is a blessing. As I walk down the hall, a woman shuffles by me in her wheelchair. She looks lost and scared. With wide eyes, she asks me, "Where am I supposed to go? What am I supposed to be doing?" She repeats these questions every time she passes me. I respond with what I hope to be soothing words. But her mind cannot make sense of what I'm saying. What, I wonder, must it be like to live in a constant state of uncertainty and panic.

I visit Vivian. She keeps questioning why she is here. She wants to go home. She tells me her children don't visit, but I'm guessing that is not true. After all she doesn't remember me from one visit to the next. She tells me there's something wrong with her head, she can't think straight. And she hopes she will get better soon. Vivian is not frightened like the woman in the hall. Her awareness comes and goes and she finds reasons to smile in between.

Mr. P. is in the stage where awareness of something being wrong has been replaced with "just being" in the moment. And while that presents its own frustrations at times, it appears to be a less frightening place to be. Mr. P. is not one of my hospice patients. He is the father of a man I know, so I visit him, too. He cannot remember me. I re-introduce myself each time. And he is always happy to "meet" me. Mr. P. loves to talk about soccer. He's been playing for 80 years he tells me one day. "In fact, I have a game this afternoon."

At times he gets agitated. One day he points at a staff person and says, "That guy doesn't know what he's doing." and "Why isn't he taking me out; he said he would." That much he has right. "That guy" is the activities person and he is taking patients down one at a time to the activity room where they will paint. "Don't worry, Don," he says cheerily to Mr. P. "I'll be right back to get you." I've watched "that guy" interact with the patients. He is wonderful with them. He looks to be in his twenties and I think what an amazing gift for someone so young. To get his mind off the fact that he is "being ignored", I ask Mr. P. about soccer. His eyes brighten up as he tells me a coaching story and I am rewarded with his beautiful smile.

It is sad to know that this stage too, when one can still engage with the people around him, will pass. To a place where jumbled memories reveal themselves in disconnected sentences, like Dolly. And worse still, to withdrawing almost completely from a world that no longer holds anything worth opening ones eyes for, like June.

❦

Pearl

She's not one of my hospice patients, but I pass Pearl often in my visits and have wanted to stop and talk to her. So far I haven't. She can barely communicate and I don't know how to approach her. But one day as I was leaving the facility I couldn't get her out of my mind. Her eyes seemed to be pleading for attention. I vowed to go back the next day to spend time with her.

When I returned the following day, Pearl was in the hallway in her wheelchair. I lowered myself to her level. I told her who I was. "My husband knew you when you did Hospice work together." I couldn't hear even a whisper, but I could read Pearl's lips. "I don't remember him," she said "but please tell him I said hello." "I will." She said more, but I told her, "I'm so sorry, Pearl. I can't understand what you're saying." She tried several more times; again I apologized. And she said, "It's my fault. It's my fault." I was touched by her response. She didn't get frustrated or angry. She was letting me off the hook. I couldn't help but feel that there was still a vital part of Pearl that Alzheimer's had yet to take away. She was still the sweet kind lady who had once done Hospice work.

I held her hand in mine. I knew Pearl was Jewish. I began to sing a little Jewish song I'd learned with the Hospice choir. She held tight to my hand and mouthed the words as I sang. Then I sang the only other Jewish song I knew. She sang along.

When I told her I would be leaving, she said, "Please stay. Please stay." I stayed a bit longer and then asked if I could come back again. "Yes. Please come back." But when I got up Pearl leaned forward; she wanted me to help her up too. She pleaded in a whisper I could now hear, "Help me . . . help me . . . help me." As though she was imploring me to help her escape this body that would not allow her to stand up and walk away from the monotony of these halls. "Help me . . . please help me." She kept repeating. Her eyes seemed to say "Please, please free me from this mind that won't let me find the words. Please help me out of this prison."

"I'll come back, Pearl. I'll come back."

When I lay my head down that night, I could still hear Pearl saying "Help me . . . "

෨෴

I recently attended the NAMI NH Annual meeting. Besides tending to the normal "annual meeting" business, NAMI NH was also celebrating its 35th year anniversary. It started because of Peggy Straw. In 1972, Peggy's daughter had been diagnosed with a mental illness. Desperate for help and more information, Peggy sought, but was unable to find, a support group anywhere in the state. In 1978 she started her own support group. In 1979 she heard that a group of families in Wisconsin was considering forming a National Alliance for Mental Illness. Peggy wanted "in". She attended the first organizational meeting in Chicago, representing New Hampshire. In 1982 NAMI NH was legally incorporated and affiliates throughout the state were formed. Through the years, Peggy remained an advocate for the cause of serving the mentally ill and their families. In 2016, an addition built onto the office of the NAMI NH headquarters in Concord, was named the "Peggy M. Straw Hall". Peggy was present and spoke at the dedication.

Ken Norton, the current Executive Director at NAMI NH knew Peggy well. At the Annual Meeting I attended, he spoke of Peggy's unending commitment and service to NAMI. The anniversary celebration was bittersweet. Ms. Straw had died unexpectedly only two months earlier at the age of 87.

After his words honoring Peggy Straw, Ken went on to speak about House Bill 400 that had just passed and been signed into law. He presented an award to Senator Bradley who had tirelessly pushed the bill.   Among other things, the bill provides that funds be designated for 12 more beds at the NH State Hospital which provides acute, inpatient psychiatric services.   It will also fund the creation of more Mobile Crisis Units in the state. Both are sorely needed. Patients are languishing in emergency rooms awaiting an available bed.   The Mobile Crisis Units are on call 24-7 offering interventions with mentally ill persons that often prevent the need for hospitalization.

This is just the backdrop for the story Ken went on to tell us. He said that last week, on the day HB 400 passed, he headed back to his office walking on air and all he could think was "Today feels like Christmas!" When he entered his office he saw a battered envelope on his desk. It appeared to be a greeting card. It was postmarked with three different dates.   When Ken opened the envelope he found a Christmas card that had apparently been lost in the mail over the past few months, only now reaching its proper destination. Inside was written, *I didn't want you to think I forgot you.*

And was signed . . . *Peggy Straw.*

❧❧

Victoria

Victoria is one of my hospice patients. She is 103 years old. She is always dressed nicely, her slacks and sweater color coordinated. Vicky is sharp and a delight to chat with. On my first visit with her, she mentioned that she enjoyed music. I asked who some of her favorite singers were. After some thought, she said Nat King Cole. "Would you like to listen to one of his songs?" I asked. "That would be nice," she said. So I pulled up a youtube video on my notebook of him singing "Unforgettable". "My goodness," she said. "I can even *watch* him singing!"

Later visits would elicit more wonderment from Vicky at the amazing capabilities of this new technology. Sometimes a conversation would give me reason to consult my smart phone to clarify something she was unsure of. "Unbelievable!" she'd exclaim. This would lead to her talking about how so much has changed in her lifetime. How much she has seen in over 100 years. The advances in transportation for example. She spoke of accompanying her father on his delivery route. "We were riding in a horse and buggy. Actually, now that I think about it, it was a surrey, like the song . . a surrey with the fringe on top."

"You must bring your friends back to sing again. That was so delightful," she said one day. Our hospice choir had come to sing for our patients there two weeks earlier. How she enjoyed it. We surrounded Vicky and sang the old tunes. Midway through our singing, we heard a bass voice accompanying us. A gentleman resident in a wheelchair had shuffled to the doorway and joined in. When we finished, we thanked him for singing with us. He asked if we knew "I want a gal, just like the gal who married dear old dad". We sang the verse we knew, then he continued with a verse we hadn't heard . . . "I want a beer just like the beer that pickled my old dad"!

Recently, when I walked into Victoria's room to see her, the aid was just leaving. "How is she?" I asked. "Oh, Victoria's in a great mood. I just did her nails and she loves the color. She didn't like the last one I put on her." I admired Vicky's nails. They were done in a lovely, classy shade of pink. She seemed pleased until she spotted my hands. "Oooo, I really like your nails. I like them better than mine!" she said. No matter how much I declared her color beautiful, she insisted it was not as nice as mine. I told her I'd let her know what brand and color mine was.

A few days later I brought my bottle of polish and told her she could keep it. She thanked me and said she couldn't wait to have her nails redone. "Have a chocolate," Victoria said pointing to the box on her bureau. There were only four left. I passed the box to her. After she chose hers, I took one. Victoria bit into hers. She appeared to be enjoying it, then asked me, "What kind did you get?" "Orange filled." I said. "Oh, orange is my favorite. Do you think there are any more in there?" The others were of a different shape than mine. "I don't think so." I told her. She threw the rest of her first chocolate in the waste basket and tried another anyway. She wasn't certain what it was. "Well, it might be orange." She tried to convince herself.

They say that sometimes other people are like a mirror, reflecting back to us traits that we don't really like in ourselves. In Vicky I saw myself. How many times have I bought something for the house only to see "something better" a few weeks later, and wish I'd bought *that* one. Or been out for dinner with my husband or a friend and looked at what they'd ordered and wished I had ordered the same thing. If I don't learn to be content with what I have and not be so caught up in such trivial disappointments, in my 90's I'll still be wishing I'd chosen the *other* chocolate!

തൈ

Shine on Harvest Moon

While chatting with the hospice patients on the non-dementia units is easy, it can be difficult making that one-on-one connection with some of my Alzheimer people. Before visiting the Alzheimer floor last week, I asked myself how I could best reach them.

Often the patients are gathered in the hallway in their wheelchairs. It allows them to be less isolated and gives those who are able, the freedom to "walk" along the hallways using their feet to move themselves. I decided to sing to them. With lyric sheets in hand, I asked the nurses if that was okay. "Of course." they said.

So I stood in the hallway amongst the patients (three of my hospice patients among them) and just sang. To all of them. The old songs. A few didn't respond. But most of them did. Smiles appeared. Voices joined in, the lyrics still part of their memory. For that half hour, music somehow connected us all. Even some of the staff could be heard singing along.

❧❧

Aunt Doris
(late summer)

Working in hospice has exposed me to people whose lives are in their final chapters. A chapter that may not have played out the way they would have chosen . . . dementia, cancer, loneliness, wheelchairs, frailty. My own parents died before any of those things took control of their lives. Dad died of a heart attack at the wheel of the car. And though Mom was beginning to show signs of dementia, heart disease took her quickly before Alzheimer's fully claimed her memory. Roby's parents died before old age. Neither of us experienced having to place one of our parents in a nursing home.

For many years, Roby has been looking after his Aunt Doris. She and her husband, Paul had never had children. She has a niece, June in Massachusetts, who she is very close to and another niece in Maine. Roby looks out for Doris' welfare, keeps her home in good repair and manages her finances. He had promised his Uncle Paul he would do that. But, I know my husband. He would have done it anyway. Just as he did for two other elderly Aunts . . . just because.

Until recently Doris still lived on her own. Though physically she needed a walker to walk safely in her home and wore an alert button around her neck, at ninety-three years old, Doris was still sharp as a tack. She loved to read. Not fluffy romance novels, but non-fiction, historical biographies and the NY Times. She loved watching the Red Sox and the Patriots, though it seemed the sport itself was less important than the hot young players. Doris may have been old, but not to old to appreciated a good looking guy.   After a minor car accident, she was quite enamored with the young policeman who showed up. During a stint in the emergency room after a fall, Doris mentioned more than once that the EMT who had come to assist her was not bad to look at!

Doris had a great sense of humor and enjoyed Roby's sarcastic kidding.   After her hair appointment, he'd tell her, "Well, I guess it's cheaper than plastic surgery." "He treats me more like I'm his sister than his aunt!" she'd say, suggesting she got no respect.

With an occasional "tweak" to make everyday living a little easier for her, Doris was able to continue life in her home. Meals on Wheels alleviated her need to cook. A woman came to do Doris' laundry, take her food shopping and to the hairdresser. Every morning Roby would go to her house to fill her Kuerig coffee machine, get her mail from the day before and check in on her. She was usually still asleep and unaware of him peeking in her bedroom to make sure she was okay. Roby had only recently bought Doris the Keurig. She loved it. After a couple weeks, she expressed her wonderment that it never ran out of water! Roby enlightened her. "I fill it every morning, Aunt Doris."

A few weeks ago, during his routine morning check, Roby found her lying on her kitchen floor. Fully dressed from the day before, she'd apparently been there all night. "Are you okay, Aunt Doris?" He would wonder at the absurdity of that question later. Of course she wasn't okay! She was lying on the floor! But she answered, "I'm okay". "Why didn't you press your alert button?" "I didn't feel like it; I'm comfortable here."

Previous falls had always prompted her to push her alert button and seek help right away. This one was different. Like her other falls, she hadn't broken anything and wasn't in pain. But this time, she wasn't thinking clearly.

Tests revealed a mass at the back of her brain. It appeared to be a tumor and we were told the prognosis wasn't good. Surgery at her age would be dangerous, and the loss of her quality of life from the operation alone could not justify the risk. After several days in the hospital Doris was moved to a nursing home for skilled care.

Doris has good days and bad days. Days when she is sitting up in a wheelchair. Days when she'd rather just lie in bed. She eats very little. Mentally, Doris slips in and out of reality, sometimes from one moment to the next. She'll talk about how she doesn't understand why she is unable to do what she did before, but that she likes the nurses and they take good care of her. She'll mention the fact that perhaps she won't be able to go back home. These truths, she is seemingly aware of. In the next breath, she'll say things that are incoherent. One minute the Doris we know is smiling and kidding with us. Then confusion sets in and her comments make little sense. She asked Roby how her father was doing. Her father's been gone over sixty-five years. Roby said, "not well."

As we navigate this new territory, a journey many of our friends are on with their parents, we are faced with decisions that we'd hoped Doris would have been able to make herself. She'd fallen three times in the past year. Though unable to get back up, she'd broken no bones. Roby hinted at assisted living; Doris avoided the subject. I love my home, she'd said.   Now the choice had been taken away from her.   Given the prognosis along with Doris' impaired reasoning, Roby followed the wishes in her living will and made the decision to forgo surgery and let nature take its course.   When Medicare coverage ends, we may soon have to decide whether to sell her home to pay for her nursing care.   These decisions don't come without a measure of guilt.

"I know this isn't what you wanted, Aunt Doris.   I know you wanted to live in your house the rest of your life."   I let her know I understand what she must be feeling.   But, I can't really imagine what it must be like to be okay one day, and suddenly find yourself in a nursing home, unwell, unable to care for yourself, knowing you can't go back to your home.

"It *is* nice having people helping me.   They're good to me," she says.   And I wonder if she really believes this or is trying to convince herself.   Still, I allow myself to be comforted by her words.   Believing that she is comfortable here takes away some of the guilt.

෧෧

Dad and His Pigeons

During my morning walk, I sometimes notice pigeons on a house several blocks away. Common in the downtown parks, but a bit unusual in our suburban neighborhood. I wonder if they are "homers" and I'm reminded of my father. Ever since I was little, Dad had raised and raced homing pigeons. He'd let them out every day and they would always return, landing on the roof of our house before coming down back to the coop. To train his birds for races, he'd crate them and drive to rural areas, where he'd let them go. They'd often get back home before Dad. Before a bird would be put in a race, a rubber ring with an identification number would be placed on its leg. All the club members entering their birds had a special clock to record the time the birds returned from a race. Each member's clock was calibrated to reflect the exact distance from the point of the beginning of the race (where the birds were let go) to the member's home. From New Hampshire, a truck would bring the pigeons to the start point of the present race. There was a 200 mile race, a 300, and so on. The furthest one I recall was to somewhere in Ohio, some 600 miles away.

Dad could guess approximately when the birds might return. He would sit in the backyard waiting anxiously for the first of his birds to appear. But showing up on the roof to our house meant nothing until the pigeon returned to the coop, where Dad could remove the rubber ring and place it in the clock to be recorded. I can remember Dad cursing birds that refused to come down from the roof. Sometimes winning a race was determined by seconds. He couldn't afford to have a pigeon taking his sweet time!

Cats were the enemy. A neighbor's cat in the yard would only be tolerated so many times. They sometimes disappeared. We kids never asked what happened to them, though we suspected they'd been taken for a long ride, or worse. Dad also didn't appreciate city pigeons that showed up on our roof. He would scare them away, calling them "bums". Though a quiet sweet man by nature, Dad's patience grew thin with anything that interfered with his pigeon races. I never fully appreciated Dad's hobby. We just took it for granted. Now I wish I'd asked him how he'd gotten started.

A year after Dad died I met a man, somewhat younger than me, named John at a local bank. He was the banker helping Lou and me with some financial business. Somehow my maiden name was mentioned. "Labrie? I knew a man with that name. Where did you live?" When I told him the west side of Manchester in Pinardville, he said, "That's where I met him. My uncle lived in the house behind his. Mr. Labrie had homing pigeons." When I told him that was my father, he related how he'd been so intrigued by Dad's hobby and had asked Dad all about raising the birds and racing them. "He got me started. He gave me some young birds to raise." I had never known about John. How I wished Dad was still alive so I could tell him I'd met him and what Dad's kindness had meant to him.

Dad took a few reprieves from pigeons over the years, but always went back to it. He was 76 years old when he took his birds for a final ride. He died of a heart attack at the wheel of his car, on a rural road ten miles from home, a crate of pigeons in the rear of the wagon. After his funeral, Mom collected the racing trophies and ribbons Dad had accumulated over the years and gave them out to the grandchildren. A little part of Pepere to take home with them.

৯৯৯

I'm Becoming My Mother

I have often been told (by aunts and uncles and older cousins) that I look just like my mother. Whenever we'd cross paths, my cousin Marcel would always greet me with "ma tante Faith!" (Aunt Faith in French). As a young adult, I hated hearing it. Now not so much.

I will soon be 65 years old. I didn't realize that one *had* to apply for Medicare upon reaching 65. That is, until my current medical insurance company notified me that as of November 1st, they would no longer be my primary medical insurance -- I must apply for Medicare, fill out and return the enclosed form with a copy of my Medicare card attached. What Medicare card? Really?

My mother died when she was 74 and my most vivid memories of Mom are of her in her 60's. I can't believe I'm there. Not that I haven't noticed the signs. The flabby (or flappy) underarm skin. The beginnings of jowls. The wrinkles. The dark spots on my hands. Having to cross my legs when I sneeze. My head of silver hair, which for some reason I don't see in the mirror, but shows up in photographs!

Physical changes we don't have much control over, but behavior is another thing. So senior status didn't really hit me until yesterday when I decided to use one of those 7 day pill organizers. I take one prescription medication, (a low-dose blood pressure med that I took sparingly the first year because I insisted I didn't need it, but now realize I do) the rest are supplements. As I counted and dropped the pills in each slot, I turned to

Roby and said, "Well, this is it. I'm becoming my mother. Not only am I wearing my reading glasses on a rope (which I resisted for a long time because my mother always wore her glasses that way), I'm also using a pill box!"

❧❧

Remembering Doris

Less than eight weeks after a brain tumor brought Doris down, she died quietly during the night. The last week, we noticed her rapid deterioration. The day before she died, she didn't recognize us. The next day she didn't open her eyes, her irregular breathing a sign that she was nearing the end. We held vigil most of the day, finally leaving to go home and rest. It would be our last time with her alive.

Roby had asked Doris many times over the last couple of years, to make her funeral arrangements or at least let us know what she would want when the time came. She planned to live to 100, so I guess she figured she had plenty of time. Her state of mind after the fall prevented us from having the conversation once she was in the nursing home. Knowing her time was short, Roby had gone ahead and met with a funeral director just two weeks before to make the plans we knew she would have wanted: a wake and a Catholic Mass at St. Joseph's Cathedral where she'd attended Mass and sung in the choir.

Doris and Paul had been active politically and socially. And considering her age and the fact that many of her acquaintances were gone, the funeral was well attended. Roby gave a beautiful eulogy that was both humorous and touching.

Walking through Doris' house was different after she died. Her absence was felt as we walked through each room looking at all the things we'd have to find a new home for. There was little here that Roby and I wanted to keep. At a stage where we are trying to rid ourselves of our own things, we don't need anything new. A little keepsake, perhaps, to remember her by. Her niece, June requested only the watercolor painting she'd given Doris years ago. And maybe a watch. I chose a lovely bracelet. Michael, who had developed a relationship with Doris over the past few months, had visited her often at the nursing home. He chose two small pottery cups and took some towels.

I've begun to compile names and numbers of places that we can donate things to. Dishes, pots and pans and some furniture to an organization that helps new refugees set up housekeeping. Old towels to an animal shelter. Warm sweaters and clothes to a homeless shelter. Other clothing to a local thrift shop.

We came upon some old photo albums. Doris had said that her husband Paul loved taking pictures of her. One album attested to that. A picture of Doris cooking, of Doris working in the garden, Doris ironing, Doris with a laundry basket, Doris reading . . .

Sadly there were old photos of people that neither Roby nor June could identify. Their significance in the family unknown, many were thrown out. There were other things that raised questions in my mind, that Doris was no longer here to answer. I wondered when she had gotten the beautiful china set in her closet and had she used it much. We discovered a shoebox containing four old dolls. I have a picture of my mother (who would be Doris' age) holding a doll when she was a child. These dolls looked far older. Could they have belonged to Doris' mother? The answer to that and many other questions, we will never know.

The morning of her funeral I pulled up some pictures I'd taken of Doris the day of the Luau. These were the best memories we had of Doris at the nursing home. What a festive event it was. Each person attending received a lei around their neck. Tables were set up outdoors. A load of beach sand had been brought in with pails and shovels for the kids. Hawaiian dancers. Music. A food buffet. Roby and I had headed to Villa Crest doubtful that Doris would even feel up to going outside, let alone eat anything. After all, since she'd been there, she'd gone back and forth, good days, bad days. Most days barely eating. But we'd give it a try.

To our surprise, Doris was already outside. The nurses had put her wheelchair at a table with two other patients. She had her multi colored top on with a lei to match. She was in high spirits. The pictures I took of her that day bring a smile. One of her eating a hot dog. Guzzling a can of soda. I even have a short video of her swaying her shoulders to the song: *Girl from Ipanema.* Another of her singing along to an old song. That day was a gift. She would have no other days as good as that one. There would be few days in the coming weeks that were good at all.

One of the few things that Doris enjoyed the last two weeks was the chocolate frappe that Roby would bring her every day. She couldn't put any food down. But she loved those frappes. He began to bring one for her roommate too and made a fast friend. I knew Doris enjoyed classical music. The nurses brought in a radio and I put on the classical station for her. She would close her eyes and move her hands as if directing. One day we arrived to find Doris with a stuffed elephant in her arms. Michael asked her, "Where did the elephant come from, Aunt Doris?" "Oh, he just walked in," she answered with a chuckle. She never lost her sense of humor. These are the memories that bring a smile . . . now that Doris is gone.

જ્જ

Warriors

Driving cancer patients, I've met people of all ages and different races. Some are chatty, some cannot speak English. I've picked them up at drug recovery facilities, low-income housing and wealthy neighborhoods. They live alone; they have spouses who work and can't take time off for the daily radiation treatments; they are old and frail; they are younger than my sons. Cancer makes no distinction.

Sometimes they ask me if I'm a survivor. I tell them, no I've never had cancer. We all know someone, likely many someones, who've had cancer. Some are survivors, some not. I wake up each morning grateful for my health; knowing that that can change in a heartbeat.

Surprisingly, many of the patients I drive are upbeat, but I also see faces that can't hide the exhaustion, weariness and sometimes despair that weeks or months of treatments can bring. They are fighting a battle they did not volunteer for, but are struggling hard to win. They are warriors.

ॐॐ

Cleaning House

Cleaning out Aunt Doris' house was a reminder that my own home needed some serious decluttering. Specifically the basement. Besides a fair amount of my own things that need to be gone through, it is still home to many of my boys' belongings. In the past, efforts to get rid of some of their things were met with resistance. One year I pulled out a large suitcase filled with stuffed animals.

"Okay, guys. It's time to do something with these."

One by one I pulled them out. My sons, now grown men, still managed to find sentimental reasons why they should be kept.

"Pooh Bear! He was my favorite!"

"You bought me Brown bear when I was sick!"

"I bought Possum at school in third grade!"

"My friend gave me that bunny!"

"Oh wow, I forgot about Polar bear!"

Despite their enthusiasm and attachment, they had no intention of taking them home, of course.

Musical instruments from the boys' high school band days were, for several years after they moved out, still used occasionally when they were all home. I enjoyed the jam sessions. But now the drums and guitars have sat unused for years. My numerous suggestions to pass these on have fell on deaf ears.

On his last visit home, I handed David a box filled with his old cassettes and CD's. As his eyes opened wide excitedly looking over his old treasures, his wife Leliah looked at him and said, "Don't even think about it! We don't have room for them in our small apartment!"

Then there are the boxes of college papers and text books, photos, comic book collections and baseball cards. And really, when they are home, I hate to have the boys spend what little time we have together, going through their things.

Working at Doris' house has put the bug in me to finally attack my basement and I've come up with a solution. I take pictures of several items at a time and e-mail the pictures to the boys asking them to give me a "Yes" "No" or "Maybe I'd like to see it one more time before deciding". So far, it's working. They've said *no* more than *yes* and a handful of *maybe's*. Old text books, comic collections, special t-shirts, school art projects and miscellaneous other items have either been deep sixed or passed on.

I took a group picture of all their stuffed animals and sent it on to them with this message: "Take one last look at your childhood friends before I find a new home for them!" They responded with "goodbye old pals" and "farewell little buddies", and David's "Can I keep Beary, though?" Well, David *is* the youngest.

I still have a long ways to go, but with the boys several years further removed from their things, the attachment to them has lessened. It's becoming clearer to me what sort of things hold sentimental value to them and which things they are happy to part with. This knowledge will make going through the boxes of things *I've* saved over the years an easier task. I've held on to items from their childhood that I assumed the boys would want and am beginning to realize they probably won't!

&⋘

The Writing Circle

I joined the Circle because it was being run by Jackie, my Hospice choir co-director, who I enjoy working with and Gail, a woman whose path I've crossed many times through hospice and who I would love to get to know better. And the Circle intrigued me. It was being offered to Life Journey volunteers. Though I had not yet joined the program, Jackie invited me to "just come and check it out". She had said more than once that Life Journey was perfect for me. I figured this was her way of roping me in.

The Life Journey program has been on my radar ever since I first heard of it. It is an opportunity for a Hospice volunteer to meet one on one with a patient who would like to have his or her memories, stories or letters written down for the family he or she will leave behind. I love to write, and until now, I'd felt unprepared for the patient interaction that doing this would require. But having done nursing home visitations the past few months, I feel ready.

Of course, I had no idea what the writer's circle would entail. We're doing a book called "Your Write to Heal". The idea is, that if we can tap into our own "hard stuff" and past stories, perhaps we'll be better able to work with the Life Journey patients. Our first meeting in October simply laid out the plan for the coming months. We would continue to meet once a month after having read one chapter. Each chapter had multiple exercises to do. The author strongly encouraged 20 minutes of writing each week. Several meditations were also part of the assignment.

"I had a hard time with the first chapter." I said at our November meeting.

"I didn't know what to write. It talks about looking back on all the bad things in our childhood. Looking at things we haven't gotten past, or haven't dealt with, people we haven't forgiven. I had a good childhood. The things I thought my parents could have done better, I've long ago forgiven, realizing they did the best they could. And I always felt loved. What's to write about?"

There were seven of us that day. Some had some issues they still needed to reconcile. Others in the group spoke of hardships growing up, but had no lasting wounds. "Surely, you had *something* in your youth that was difficult?" The question was directed at me.

"Well, I had a nervous breakdown when I was 12. But I don't think about it anymore." I said.

"Now that's huge!" Jackie said.

"What do you think brought it on?" another asked.

Until a NAMI meeting three years ago, I'd never spoken of this to anyone. And I hadn't since. Everyone else had shared. It was my turn.

"I don't know for sure. I just remember lying in bed one night thinking how I was almost a teenager. That I was going to be an adult in just a few years and I would have to leave the comfort and security of my family and my home. I guess I became overwhelmed with a fear of growing up.

"It was debilitating. I missed weeks of school. I remember spending days in bed. I wanted someone in the room with me every minute; if left alone, I was afraid I'd stop breathing. Eventually I went back to school. But fears followed me into high school. I was shy and insecure." I went on to tell them how, as a young adult, I suffered panic attacks, my heart racing, my palms sweating and being certain that I was going to die. That I never even told my first husband about these attacks. I figured he'd think I was crazy. Back then I didn't know that what I was experiencing had a name. I'd never heard of "panic attacks".

I told them, "Marrying Lou and having children gave me confidence and purpose. I stopped having panic attacks but would still be fearful whenever Lou was away on a business trip and I was alone with the kids. I was afraid something awful would happen. But I couldn't stand feeling this way and learned how to deal with my fearful thoughts, by pushing them away every time they entered my mind. It took time and a lot of practice, but I did this over and over until I finally conquered it. I guess this is what they now call cognitive behavioral therapy."

When I'd been reading the exercise assignments at home, I thought it silly to wrack my brain trying to find some darkness in my past. "What am I suppose to do ... make something up?" I asked myself. I could see no benefit in doing the exercise. The book was meant for someone who had some serious stuff to deal with. I was certain I'd have nothing to say at the group discussion. I was wrong. While the healing had taken place years ago, it was liberating to speak freely of that time. And to recognize that the strength I found within me to deal with my fears years ago, continues to serve me when I need it most.

❧

Friends

Thanksgiving is just around the corner. There are many things I'm thankful for... health, financial security, etc. but what I am most thankful for is the relationships in my life. Family is at the top of the list, but friends are right up there, too.

Throughout our lives, we seek to surround ourselves with those who nurture our growth and well-being. We let go of the people who don't, those who bring us down or whose lifestyles and morals conflict with our own. We are discerning without being judgmental. We choose people who we enjoy spending time with. People who have something to teach us. People we share a common interest with. People who accept us as we are. These are the people we call "friends".

Some friends come and go; others last a lifetime. While some people maintain relationships with childhood friends their whole lives, others, like myself, have long ago lost touch with the kids they shared the playground with. As our personalities matured, we may have grown away from our best buddies from elementary school.

Friendships emerge from connections made with people who share our interests or whose lives (at least for a time) parallel our own. Mothers at the soccer field, coworkers, parents of our kids' friends, etc. Unless a close bond has been formed, we spend little time with these "temporary" friends once that common thread no longer exists. This doesn't make these friendships any less valuable. These relationships served us well at the time. And though the only time you speak to these friends nowadays is when you bump into them at the supermarket, you still enjoy seeing them.

Am I using the word "friend" too loosely? I don't think so. Not every friend we have is of the bosom buddy, let me share my problems with you variety. Some are what we'd call "casual" friends. But each friendship, whether close or casual, has value and allows us to learn something about ourselves in the give and take process of being a friend.

I find that each of my friends is unique and I get something different from each one. One friend is on a spiritual path that parallels my own and we are mutually enriched by conversations on this subject. Another is more like family, a sister, the one with whom I've shared happy and sad times over the years. There are friends who are always available for a cup of tea and a chat. There is my "ready for anything" friend who can always be counted on to do something spontaneous. And there are the wonderful women I've met through Hospice with whom I share a special bond.

Each friend is a treasure, a gift. And I give thanks.

ॐ∾ॐ

The Bottle

When I got the water bottle from Colette for Christmas I said, "This is great! I have a smaller one just like it and I've been wanting a bigger one."

It did seem a bit larger than what I'd wanted, though. A few days later when I took all my gifts that remained in their original boxes from under the tree, I looked at the bottle again. It was a glass water bottle with a turquoise silicone sleeve; it matched my smaller version. I wondered if I should just tell Colette it was larger than I really needed. Maybe she could exchange it. Maybe I shouldn't say anything. It was just so big!

When I went to bed I was still indecisive about returning the bottle. It *was* a thoughtful gift. But I probably wouldn't use it. The more I thought about it, the more I pictured it, the bigger the bottle became in my mind. By the time I awoke in the morning the bottle was the size of a 5 gallon gas can.

Later I pulled out my stainless steel water bottle. The one I no longer use because I lost its cap. I filled it with water, then poured *that* water into the one Colette had given me. The water came exactly to the top. The new glass bottle held the same amount of water as my old stainless steel one!

We often do that with problems, too, don't we? We let our imaginations create negative scenarios that have no real basis. But we allow ourselves to believe them, and our problems grow way out of proportion. They can seem insurmountable when we let worries and fears run rampant in our minds.

Before you let your problem turn into a 5 gallon gas can, quiet your mind and have faith in your ability to handle whatever comes your way. Replacing our fears with a belief that every problem has a solution can invite clarity about what our next step should be. Just talking about your problem with someone can give you a change in perspective . . . maybe even make you realize your problem isn't as "big" as you thought it was.

కుింర

2018

Youth is the gift of nature,
but age is a work of art.

Stanislaw Jersey Lec

Still Alive

Roby and I recently attended a conference geared towards health professionals and volunteers in the hospice and palliative care fields. Talk of the role that Hospice plays at the end stage of life reminded me of my own desire to die at home. If I end up in the hospital and prognosis is that I'm dying, I don't want to be hooked up to monitors in a hospital room with bright lights and noisy hallways. I want to go home to live my final days. Hospice allows a person to live as fully and comfortably as possible in this final stage. Hospice also takes over the role of advocate for both patient and caregivers, giving the family the support they need.

During one session, we were shown a documentary called "Living While Dying". The filmmaker, Cathy Zheutlin decided to explore death when her mother's partner was diagnosed with terminal cancer. In a five year span she would follow the lives of three more friends with terminal illnesses. What each of them had, following the shock of the reality of their illness, was the gift of time (however little) to decide how they wished to live out their final weeks or months. All four chose to spend their final days at home under hospice care.

The film was incredibly uplifting. What came through was not a fear of dying, but rather an acceptance. And with that acceptance came (as one man stated) a feeling that he was more alive now as he was dying than he'd ever been before. We watch as one gentleman dances with his wife in their living room only days before he dies. Another, a younger man, uses a stand-up comedy routine to talk about dying.

I was struck by their ability to recognize when it was time to stop treatment and let their bodies follow its natural course. I hope, should the time come, I have the wisdom to do the same. As one speaker said, "non-treatment *is* a treatment."

When my brother Ron's lung cancer returned after a few months of remission, he chose not to do treatments again. He knew the treatments would only prolong the inevitable, the effects of chemo taking away the quality of what little life he had left.

What I learned from the film and my brother, is that how one accepts his illness and his mortality directly affects those around him. From the time he first learned he had cancer, Ron was open and candid about it and I realized what a blessing this was to those of us who loved him. We didn't have to wonder what to say or how to behave around him. He had set the stage. We laughed, we cried, we reminisced; we spoke openly about our feelings. We told each other "I love you".

The intent of Zheutlin, is to encourage conversation about our end of life desires *before* we are ill, or too ill to speak for ourselves. She seeks to remove the cloud of fear we have about death and the reluctance to have an open discussion about this stage of life that should be celebrated just as every other stage of our life is celebrated. What else would I tell my loved ones?

Don't see me as "dying", see me as "living".
    As long as I am breathing . . . I am still alive;
        please treat me that way.
If I am old and wrinkled, frail and forgetful, remember:

Inside *I am still the person* who ran with her children,
who broke out in song, who laughed with friends,
who loved   not one, but two husbands and lived life
fully.
I love music; let me hear music once in a while.
If my days are limited, let me have ice cream for supper
if that's what I want.
Make me smile.
Make me laugh.
Bring back the good and funny memories.
Give me a stuffed animal to hug.
If I have Alzheimer's . . .
Remember who I was and who I still am on the
inside. (even if I can't remember who *you* are)
Remember I still have feelings.
I still need kindness (even if I'm ornery)

Until my last breath, let me *live* . . . with dignity.

৯৵৹

Guilt

Today I learned that the Tibetan language has no word for "guilt". When one does something that they regret, rather than let it consume them with guilt, the memory of that regretful action serves as a catalyst to do better in the future. Guilt is one of those useless emotions that prevents us from moving forward. It weighs heavy on us and affects our self perception. Guilt and self-loathing is prevalent in our culture. Yet it is interesting to note that in Tibetan culture there is no such concept as low self-esteem. While Tibetans do experience *regret*, they do not view that regretful action as a flaw in their character.

Regret can torture us, only if we choose to dwell on it. Thoughts of "I could've" "I should've" won't change anything. Rather than dwell on it, we can learn from it and let it go. The memory of that regretful situation will surface when faced with similar circumstances in the future and the lesson will help us to make better choices in our behavior and wiser decisions.

And remember, should'ves, could'ves are great in hindsight. But for the most part we did the best we could at the time given the circumstances we were in. So be compassionate with yourself and let it go.

భా

The Vigil

It is my second vigil as a Hospice volunteer. Sitting vigil is being present with a patient who is close to death. If a dying patient has no family left, a nursing facility may request a vigil volunteer. Sometimes it is at the request of the patient's family. They may be tired and need a break, but don't want their loved one to die alone. Or the family member may just want the support and the company of the hospice volunteer. At this vigil, the dying man's daughter is present. I sit. Make some small talk. I ask about her father. The woman is happy to talk about him.

Roby sat here with her earlier. She tells me that she was grateful for his presence. That he made her laugh. That sounds like Roby. Then she is quiet. Touches her father's hand. Rubs his forehead. Tells him she loves him. And suddenly I feel insecure, inadequate. I wish I were as comfortable and natural at this as Roby is. What do I say? What do I do? Am I helping or am I a distraction? I take a deep breath and ask myself . . . if I were sitting with my dying father, what would I want of the person with me? And I thought, I would want that person to show a gentleness towards my father.

"Do you mind?" I ask the daughter as I gently rub his arm. "Not at all," she says.   For a little while we are quiet. Then I say a prayer aloud.   When I leave, the daughter expresses her gratitude, which I can see is genuine. I know that whatever little I did . . . it was enough.

❧

A Light in the Darkness

It can be overwhelming when we stop to think of all the darkness in the world. We see people suffering with circumstances they have no control over. We feel helpless, especially when it is someone close to us. We want so badly to take their pain away and are saddened because we know we can't.

We can't take away all the darkness, but we can be a light in the darkness. The world needs beacons of light, of goodness and hope. Let yourself be one of them. Feel compassion for those in darkness, shed tears. But don't let the darkness overcome you, too.

Be a light to yourself. Be a light to those around you. The world needs your smile, your joy, your love.

☙❧

Roses

"These roses under my window
make no reference to
former roses or to better ones;
they are for what they are;
they exist with God today.
There is no time to them.
There is simply the rose; it is
perfect in every moment
of its existence."

Emerson

Be like a rose. Rejoice in who you are, just as you are, right now. Don't waste time comparing yourself to anyone else. You are unique. You are perfect.

৵৵

When one appeared to be waving, I almost raised my arm to wave back. We were driving along a highway in Arizona. We passed others. A couple embracing. One extending two arms offering flowers. Others raising their arms in praise. One appeared to be directing an orchestra. Two were "high fiving" each other. Some were young. Some were showing their age. The Saguaros populate the stretches of land and the hills we were passing in southern Arizona. They live only in the Sonoran desert. I'm not talking about an Indian tribe, of course, but the Saguaro cactus. If you use your imagination though, they almost seem human. Each one is different.

The many arms or lack of them reveal something about their age. A Saguaro doesn't grow an arm until it is 50 to 70 years old and can grow multiple arms at a time. They can live to 175 years or more. It was late April and some of them were in bloom. One stood with four outstretched arms, each arm "holding" a bouquet.

My husband, Roby and I were on the last leg of a two week trip to the Southwest. We had enjoyed beautiful hikes in Zion and Bryce, an amazing boat tour on Lake Powell and the awesome views of the Grand Canyon. From there we made our way to Rte. 66, then headed to Sedona from Flagstaff. Instead of taking the main highway I17 to Sedona, we opted for the more "scenic" 89A. Little did we know that this would entail a 17 mile,

20 mph stretch down into the canyon. What may be scenic to some, proved to be somewhat traumatic for two people with acrophobia (a fear of heights). The winding switchback road offers one hairpin turn after another; and with each curve we gasped, as the deep canyon presented itself at the road's edge. It seemed the road would never end.

When we finally arrived at our hotel, our nerves shot, my first question to the gentleman at the desk was, "Is this what we have to face to get out of Sedona?" We were relieved to hear that was not the case. From Sedona, heading south to Tucson, the landscape would become more benign.

Downtown Sedona is surrounded by beautiful red sandstone rock formations; even from below you can appreciate them and enjoy their illumination in the setting sun.

We found a wetland preserve just south of town with hiking paths around three ponds. Avid bird watchers, Roby and I visited the wetlands twice. With my SLR camera and zoom, I was able to capture seven new birds to add to my "life list".

In Tucson we spent a couple days with my friend, Gabe. Gabe and I met each other in high school. Each of us shy at the time, we gravitated to each other and have remained friends ever since. Our lives took different paths; there were a couple decades when we had little contact. I married, had kids and stayed in NH; Gabe remained single and moved to Arizona. When her mother was alive, Gabe would return to NH for a few weeks every summer. We'd get together once for dinner, catch up on one another's lives and might not see or speak to each other again until the following summer. But in the past fifteen years, we've rekindled our friendship. Gabe continued the yearly drive East even after her mother died, to visit me and another close friend in Connecticut. In recent years when she was in NH we'd plan a short trip together . . . to Acadia in Maine, or the back roads of Vermont, America's Stonehenge in Salem, to Lake Winnipesaukee or the Peterborough Playhouse in western NH. We both enjoyed photography and loved traversing country roads, capturing a bit of rural America with our cameras.

The last two years, Gabe has not been able to make the trip to New Hampshire. Her pulmonary hypertension is getting worse and she doesn't have the stamina. Even through her medical setbacks, Gabe has always remained upbeat. Hooked to her oxygen, she enjoyed driving us around Tucson. Walking zaps her energy, but sitting and driving are not a problem.

We arrived on Wednesday and spent time in downtown Tucson. Early Thursday morning, Gabe took us to Sabino Canyon. A tram brought us through the canyon, making stops along the way where passengers would disembark to take the hike back. By the time we got to the last stop, Roby, Gabe and I were the only ones left. We enjoyed a pleasant conversation with the Tram driver on the way back to the visitor center where we started.

Gabe showed us some sights in the City and then drove us through Saguaro National Park. There we enjoyed not only the Saguaros, but the prickly pear and the barrel cactus, a number of them were in bloom, much to my delight.

Gabe offered to bring us to the airport at 4:00 am on Friday. I was so grateful for that, but I knew it meant as much to her as it did to me. The hour drive meant we'd get to spend just a little more time together. As we hugged at the airport I was saddened with the realization that this may be the last time we'd see each other in person. Our hug lasted longer than usual, and I knew she was thinking it, too.

ॐॐ

Sitting With Mr. A.

Is this what dying sounds like? The humming and groan of an oxygen concentrator, the sound of classical music playing softly on the bedside radio, voices of nurses chatting in the hallway . . .

I'm sitting with Mr. Anderson in the nursing home. Sitting vigil as he gets closer to a reunion with his mother. Until her death, she'd lived here at Maple Leaf for several years herself with her son. I figure Mrs. A had to have been at least 100. Her son is 80. Two years ago I had sung with the Hospice Singers for both of them here in this room. You just don't forget a mother and son sharing a room in a nursing facility.

I look through the small pile of photos that sit on the window sill. I'm not sure who some of the people in the photos are, but most of them are of Mr. A. and his mom. And a dog. His mother looks like a happy person. In each picture she wears a beautiful smile. Several shots suggest a person who relishes life, like the one of her smiling broadly, fist in the air as she sits in the front seat of a vintage automobile.

A framed photo of a dog sits on Mr. A's tray table. Mr. A. never married, never had children. It is likely that his primary source of joy and love came from his mother and his dog.

As he lies quietly, his breathing still steady, a nurse walks in to check on him and says, "It's time to go see your mother, Jack. Millie is waiting for you." He doesn't respond to her. I wonder if he hears or comprehends what she is saying. Or is the morphine keeping him comfortably oblivious.

The nurse leaves the room. A horn beeps outside. A staff person passes in the hallway pushing a broom. Two nurses down the hall are discussing their weekend plans. A resident walks briskly by, having circled round the hallway numerous times; I'm impressed with her mobility. I look at Mr. A. sleeping peacefully, soon to be gone from this world.   And for the rest of us . . . life goes on.

ം‑ക

Welcome to the Family

"Can't it wait? The storm is getting worse."

"No, this is important."

They couldn't imagine what was important enough to venture out in this March snow storm. When he arrived, Chris handed the adoption papers to my sister Deb and her husband, Steve. He'd been talking about this for some time and now had the paperwork in hand. Deb and Steve happily signed the papers.

Every adoption is special. But this one was far from typical. Chris is 36 years old. And though he'd been calling them "Mom" and "Dad" for years, he wanted to make it official. He wanted to have their last name.

Both Chris and his sister, Tara had been put in foster care when young. Deb and Steve took in Tara as a foster child when she was five. Chris was two years old at the time and on a temporary basis they took him in as well, until a foster home could be found for him. When no longer under their care, Deb and Steve went out of their way to arrange for Chris to spend time with Tara. They also made certain that Chris spent every holiday with them. Deb and Steve adopted Tara when she was seven. They tried taking Chris in again as a foster child, but it didn't work out. Still, during those years of being bounced from one foster home to another, Deb and Steve were the only constant in Chris' life. After he grew up, Chris continued to visit Deb and Steve, where he always felt at home.

Now married for several years, and with the possibility of adopting children of his own, it is the name Lemire that Chris hopes to someday pass on to his children.

Deb, Steve, Chris and his wife stood before the judge seeking the adoption. The judge had never encountered this before. Deb and Steve explained the background to her, how they had two children of their own and had adopted three of their foster children. And how Chris had become part of their family. For his part, Chris couldn't contain his joy at the prospect of officially becoming their son. The judge was impressed and touched by their story. Afterwards, she happily obliged them when asked to be in a group picture of the occasion. When the judge stood to the side, Deb asked her to stand in the middle among them. "It's not about me," she said. "But *you* made it happen." Deb told her. With Steve's cell phone, the stenographer took the picture. A week later Chris's wife would tell Deb that Chris hadn't stopped smiling since that day.

This week Roby and I joined other family members at a special party to celebrate the adoption, and to say "Welcome to the family, Chris!"

౷∘ఈ

Outsmarted

Roby raises his arms (and his voice) in frustration. There ought to be a support group for those of us who believe we can outwit a squirrel. We need to sit with others who have endured similar frustrating scenarios. We need to share our stories and know that we are not alone. Maybe even learn how to laugh at ourselves. Goodness knows the squirrels are.

After years of successfully thwarting the resourceful little critters by hanging our seed feeders from a wire strung across the yard between two trees, one of our "friends" learns how to tight rope walk. A recent addition to the wire was a nut and seed chunk. When Roby came in and told me he'd just seen a squirrel running off with something big, I looked out the window and saw the nut chunk missing.

Don't get me wrong. I like the squirrels. I put out corn cob feeders for them. We treat them to peanuts occasionally. Roby built a squirrel nesting box a few years ago, which has been used numerous times, delighting us with the sight of baby squirrels peeking out of the opening in early spring. But I like my birds, too.

Years ago, I put up the suet feeder that hangs outside our family-room window. I had hung it from a plant bracket and the squirrel jumped from the tree to the feeder. I added a baffle dome; he perched on the bracket and hung upside down to reach the suet. So I cut the bottom off of a two liter soda bottle and pushed it over the bracket. When the squirrel jumped onto the bottle, the bottle spun around throwing the squirrel safely off. Success! This has worked for over twenty years . . . until now. Our friend will jump up on the sill and claw his way across the window screen or climb up the side corner of the house to get to the suet. The edge of the house, now badly "chewed up" by his claws, looks like it has been attacked by an army of termites.

Although we have several squirrels living in our backyard, we point to the culprit and say "Look what he's up to now," as though we are battling only one. After walking the wire to the black sunflower seed feeder, he's busily shaking it, while two more squirrels wait below for falling seeds.

"What if he's not the only one?" I ask Roby. "Maybe more than one can walk the wire and they're taking turns."

Even our hummingbird feeder isn't safe. Just when you think it can't get any worse, we discover our friend has a sweet tooth. He gleefully makes his way to the sweet water and tips the feeder, drinking and spilling the entire contents unto the ground below.

I research the squirrel problem on-line and I find my support group. As others recount their own stories, I can hear the frustration in their postings. I can feel the agony of their defeat. I've been there. And I have to laugh at the absurdity of it all.

But still in battle mode, I try to learn more about my enemy. I find out that they can jump as high as four feet from the ground and ten feet from a perch. Armed with this information, we put up a pole for one of our feeders. It is far from a possible launching pad, is too high to jump to and has a squirrel baffle three feet from the bottom of the pole.

Our efforts pay off. We cheer when we see the squirrels baffled by the baffle. We try not to get too smug. We're quite sure the little guys are figuring out how to do a cheerleader pyramid, so the one on top can topple the feeder.

❧❧

Aging

"I am appalled that the term we use to talk about aging is 'anti.' Aging is as natural as a baby's softness and scent. Aging is human evolution in its pure form."
~ Jamie Lee Curtis

How true these words are. Why is there so much emphasis on trying to push back the aging process? Of course we should take care of ourselves to promote good health. But it will not prevent us from aging. We can't go backwards, we can't remain where we are. The years go by, we age. We've been getting older since the day we were born. It is natural. It is what is supposed to happen. Why do we fear it?

When I was young I had the foolish misconception that older people "thought" like older people. How surprised I was when I discovered that at 50, 60 and now approaching 70, I'm still the same person in my mind that I was when I was 25. When I lie in a loving embrace with my husband, I don't see the lines that age has etched in his face. I see a boyish grin and a youthful twinkle in his eyes; our hearts have not been told that we're no longer young.

We *are* older, of course. As our aches and pains are quick to remind us. But we are also more content. The wisdom we've accumulated over the years is a far greater treasure than youth could ever afford us. Why not celebrate the wrinkles that bear witness to the many years we have been alive. Let our gray hair reflect the beauty of our older selves. Instead of fearing it, why not embrace the most natural thing in life . . . aging.

৯~ৎ

I've chatted with people who've lost a spouse suddenly and unexpectedly. They tell me, "you understand, you experienced the same thing." I tell them that in many ways, their loss is more difficult.

When you lose someone who's been very ill and suffering for a long time, the grieving process begins long before they die. Little by little you grieve multiple losses along the way. You begin to mourn all the things you can no longer do together. You mourn your spouse's inability to enjoy some of the simple things he so loved. It began, for me, a year before my husband Lou died. He became too weak to drive, too weak to go up the stairs to our bedroom. He slept where he was most comfortable, in his recliner. We didn't know it then. We assumed he'd get better. But I would never share our bed with him again. After a few months he would have to give up the card games with friends and family. He discovered on-line games. That, too, would eventually end, as would visiting his family in Connecticut. We'd forgotten what it was like to go out any place other than doctor's appointments or stints in the ER. Lou was in the hospital for two months leading up to his death. A few days before he died, Lou whispered "I wish I could have a cigar." How he used to love sitting in the yard enjoying the birds and the gardens while puffing on a good cigar. I wondered if that life was gone forever. My heart cried for him. For us.

At first his death was a relief. He was no longer suffering. My grief in the beginning was in the remembering and the replaying over and over again, of all the worst moments, some of them tinged with guilt --- the hindsight of knowing I could have done more, I could have done things differently. When I slowly accepted that I'd done the best I could at the time, I was able to invite the good memories. But now my grief came in heart-breaking waves of missing Lou intensely, especially at times like when, less than two months after he died, I decorated the Christmas tree for the first time without him.

But in between the tears and waves of grief, I found joy in life. I continued to socialize with my friends and family. And I didn't really mind living alone.

I know that we all experience loss and grief differently. Some cannot get past their loss, no matter what the circumstances. Still, to lose someone suddenly when there is no illness, no warning, is devastating. Your world is unexpectedly and abruptly changed forever. There is no grieving in small doses, nothing preparing you for what is to come. The shock that comes with it is debilitating.

I'm not certain how I would handle losing my husband Roby suddenly. Our lives are so intertwined, I know the void would be immense. He says that when his time comes, he hopes he goes quickly. I tell him, that I don't wish him a long illness, but I would appreciate a little time to get used to the idea, before he goes. Of course we both know, it's not in our hands.

≈∽≈

What Really Matters

During my walk this morning, I asked myself if I was doing enough service for others. I know we have to take time for ourselves, but maybe I should be doing more volunteering.

After thinking about it, I realized that it isn't necessary to look beyond where we are at any given moment for ways to give and support others. Opportunities have a way of finding us and giving us reasons to listen, to extend a hand, to offer a smile.

I remember many times when I would ask Roby how his Aunt Doris was, instead of calling her myself. Or intentionally avoided someone at the grocery store because I didn't feel like chatting. Small things, perhaps. But why be more concerned with making a difference in a big way, when we can be there for others in small ways every day.

It is more about living with awareness and mindfulness and an open heart. It is paying attention to the people in our lives and those who cross our paths. It is how we live our lives each day that makes a difference.

❦

Talents

It is unlikely I will ever write that novel I'd always hoped to write. But it doesn't seem that important now. One of my favorite authors is Rachel Naomi Remen, M.D. Her books "My Grandfather's Blessings" and "Kitchen Table Wisdom" are favorites of mine. They are her own stories, taken from her life journey. Like Rachel, I am meant, I suppose, to write what I know, what I've experienced.

I am not like my son, John. I lack the imagination to create the threads that will weave themselves into some semblance of a fiction worth reading. John on the other hand says he has numerous story ideas going through his head, but can't find the time to write them down. Oh if only!

The same can be said for my artistic ability. If you asked me to draw a cow, I wouldn't know where to begin --- give me a picture of a cow, and I can draw a reasonable resemblance. John's artistic juices flow freely across the paper with only his imagination guiding him. Which is why, whenever we play Pictionary, everyone wants John on their team!

Sometimes the "talent" we wish to have is only as good as how much time we are willing to invest in the study and practice of it. Ever since I was a child, I'd wanted to play the piano. It wasn't until I was in my 40's that I finally had the opportunity, when my husband Lou, knowing how passionately I wanted one, bought me a piano. After two years of lessons, I realized that I had no innate talent for playing the piano. Nor did I have the patience or willingness to learn. I enjoy "fooling around" on the piano, memorizing bits of songs or making up little ditties, and that is enough.

We all have different talents and gifts. Some we've always been aware of, others slowly develop over time and we only later discover. Talents encompass far more than the ability to play an instrument or paint a picture. Your gift may be anything from organizational and leadership skills to cheerfully serving others.

Don't let your gifts go to waste. To quote Wayne Dyer: "Don't die with your music still inside you."

る～ら

I Killed my Mouse

"I need a new mouse," I told Roby.

"Yeah, those things don't last very long," he said.

"Well . . . actually, it's my fault."

"Your fault?"

"I killed it. My computer's been acting up all day and I haven't been able to get anything done. I got so mad, I slammed my mouse down. Now it won't work."

It wasn't the first time I damaged something during a hissy fit. I admit it. I have a temper. It is seldom triggered by people. Rather it is set off by mundane things. Like the time the lower kitchen cabinet door refused to stay closed. Using my hand I closed it only to have it pop open again. And again. And again. My patience thinning with every attempt, I finally kicked it hard with my foot. I guess I taught that door a lesson. I'd kicked it right off the hinges. I knew immediately I'd have to tell Roby. There was no logical reason for a door to just fall off it's hinges leaving the hinges bent out of shape.

I knew that Roby wouldn't be upset. He'd laugh. It was a bit of trivia he'd keep in his back pocket. Ammunition to use next time I kid him about something stupid *he* does.

It's great being married to someone with a sense of humor. Once, I hit the right edge of the garage as I was driving in. Roby claimed it sounded like a bomb had hit the house and said I must have been going awfully fast!

He exaggerates. Then again, the door would no longer close. The next day when I returned from an errand, he'd taped up a big red arrow on the garage pointing to the entrance. Very funny, Roby.

Not too long ago, only a week after getting my new car, I was backing out and scraped my front right bumper on a rock that we'd placed in the landscaping near the end of the driveway.

"It's just a little scrape," I told him.

"Little? I wouldn't call that little!" he said when he saw it.

"Well," I said, "we should probably move that rock. It's too close to the edge. Next winter, when the snow falls, we won't be able to see it."

A week later Roby and I were leaving the house . . . Roby driving. As he turned the wheel to back into the street, we heard it, that awful scraping sound.

"You didn't move that rock yet, did you?" I asked.

"Nope."

I just smiled.

☙❧

Protocol

The first time I sat to meditate with a group, I wondered what the protocol was. Did everyone close their eyes during meditation? I wanted to open my eyes to see. I felt a tickle in my throat. What if I had to cough? Should I stifle it? Would it be disrespectful to break the silence? Should I leave the room? As I tried to find a comfortable position in my chair, I wondered if those beside me could sense my movement. I didn't want to annoy anyone. Even though I knew it was silly to be so insecure (this was a Buddhist meet-up, after all) . . . I was anyway.

A few weeks later, ten minutes into our 25 minute meditation, there was a knock at the door. I knew the facilitator would go see who it was. But I was curious. Were the others still meditating or was I the only one still closing my eyes. When I peeked, I found half of them had opened their eyes and were acknowledging the latecomer with a welcoming smile.

I knew then, that there would be no one judging me if I coughed or sneezed; no one would question how I sat or whether I meditated with eyes open or closed. Why, then should I judge myself?

I realized too, that the sacredness lies, not so much in the silence, but in opening our hearts to each moment, whether it be to the quietness of our breathing or to the addition of another member to the meditation circle.

ॐॐ

Vigil

When I arrive to sit with the dying man, I am told it won't be long. The vigil team has been called in because he has no family except for a significant other who has recently been hospitalized because of her own health issues. The hospice chaplain has been sitting with him all afternoon, staying until a vigil volunteer could come. Also present is a male nurse, who has been compassionately staying with the man as much as he could when no one else was there for him. "I don't want him to die alone," he said.

The man is only 67. His breathing is erratic, a sign that he is close. I hold his hand. His dark skin is smooth. And his graying curly hair is soft to the touch. He would look peaceful if it wasn't for the labor of his breathing.

There are no pictures in the hospital room. No cards. What kind of life did he live, I wondered. I supposed it didn't really matter. At this moment, he was simply . . . a dying man. In the end, in those final moments, aren't we all the same? When death is waiting patiently to claim our last breath, is it any different for a person who is wealthy or one who is homeless, for one surrounded by family or one who is not?

After an hour, I notice it's been a few minutes since he has taken a breath, but I can still see a pulse in his neck. His head relaxes more and his pulse is getting weaker and weaker. The male nurse approaches. I think he's almost gone, I tell him. The nurse listens to his heart and nods.

It is at that moment that I hear a female nurse questioning a young woman, accompanied by a man, standing at the door. "I'm sorry, there was no mention of a daughter", the nurse is saying.

I stand, the male nurse exchanges a look with the female nurse and the daughter knows it is too late. She goes to the man's bedside and cries when she sees that her father is gone.

We give the daughter her space and the nurses thank me as I leave. It is the first time that the patient dies while I am at a vigil. I don't feel sad because of the man's passing so much as for the young woman. I wonder about her relationship with her father. Has she been in her father's life right along? If so, why was there no mention of her? Was there something unresolved between the woman and her father? Are there unspoken words? Had she hoped to hear him say "I love you" or "I'm sorry"? Had she hoped to say those words herself?

ॐ∽ॐ

Retiring

Often over the years, real estate agents or interested buyers have approached me inquiring about our 24 unit apartment building. It is in a nice neighborhood that boasts many older expensive homes and a lovely park. I've always been quick to say "Sorry, I'm not ready to sell." I knew eventually I would get there. And in the past couple years, I've found myself thinking about it more and more.

It has been forty years since my first husband, Lou bought the building. And twenty-five years since he turned it over to me to manage. When I married Roby, he enthusiastically took charge of the day to day needs of running the building. I continued to do the bookkeeping, interviewing and screening prospective tenants, and doing things at the building when needed.

The thought of no longer having the responsibility of 24 tenants was becoming more and more appealing. But it wasn't until we got our first snow storm at the end of November, that I knew the time had come. I looked out at the snow and said to Roby, "I wonder what it's like to wake up on a snowy morning, and not have to worry about whether the parking lot at the apartment building is safe. Not have to call tenants to remind them to move their cars. Not have to worry about whether a tenant will slip on an icy patch. I don't want the responsibility of it anymore. I'd like to know how it feels to simply enjoy a beautiful snowfall. I'm ready to sell. I am SO ready."

All Roby said was, "Call the realtor. Call Kim."

"Are you sure you want to sell?" Kim asked. "I know you've owned the building a long time. Are you sure you wouldn't rather turn it over to a management company?"

I insisted I was ready to sell. But when Kim brought along a fellow realtor and co-owner of a property management company, and we discussed both selling and management, I began to see the benefits of letting a management company take over.

Not the least of which, was that putting off selling would give me time to separate myself emotionally from the business. The fact is, I love my tenants. Roby and I have a great relationship with all of them. So though I'm relinquishing the responsibility, as owner I still have some input with certain tenant issues.

The decision was made and paperwork signed. The first of January, the management company will take over the running of our building. The maintenance, the collection of rents, paying of bills, filling vacancies, dealing with complaints.

We told all the tenants personally. The reaction was understandable. They're worried about increased rents, of course, but mostly they said they'll miss us. Especially Roby. They loved seeing him around the building and chatting with him. He was always there if they needed a hand with something. So, it doesn't come without mixed emotions. I'm happy with my decision, and like most people who retire, we won't miss the responsibility, but we'll miss the interaction.

The building is only two miles down the road. I don't suppose it would hurt to stop in and say hi once in a while . . .

ॐॐ

Wanting Nothing

There are different ways to interpret "wanting nothing". It can simply mean to be satisfied and grateful for what you have. But another context in which I am reminding myself to want nothing, is to, for example, not want another person to always agree with me, not want kudos when I've done something good, to not want or "need" things to be a certain way or have a certain outcome.

"Wanting" sets us up for disappointment. When I tell myself "want nothing", I relax. When you let go of "wanting", you release the need to be right, the need to understand why, the need for perfection in yourself and others, the need for more. And a magical thing happens. You are more content. You are better able to embrace life as it happens, *however* it happens.

"Want nothing".

That is my mantra as I begin 2019.

৯৹৶

Acknowledgements

*Thank you, Carol, for your friendship and support
and for correcting my paper!
Thank you, Michael, John and David,
for the wonderful conversations that I so treasure
and for your support and love.
Thank you, Roby, for teaching me a lot about
loving fully and unconditionally.
I couldn't have asked for a better companion
to share the rest of my life with!*

*For all the people who touch my life,
some in big ways, some in small,
some for a lifetime,
some for only a moment,
I am also thankful.*

Namaste
(the light in me honors the light in you)

The Stories

Made in the USA
Middletown, DE
05 February 2019